LATE SUMMER OF 1941 AND MY WAR WITH JAPAN

Weldon Hamilton 20 years old in San Francisco
September 1941

LATE SUMMER OF 1941 AND MY WAR WITH JAPAN

WELDON HAMILTON

To order additional copies of this book, contact:
Xlibris Corporation
1-888-7-XLIBRIS
www.Xlibris.com
Orders@Xlibris.com

CONTENTS

Introduction

I am writing this story as an autobiography. I made six hours of tapes some 15 years ago. It is a story of a 20-year-old boy living it 55 years ago with all the history and excitement of World War II. Because it is an autobiography of long ago there is always the possibility of an error in memory. As one famous Union general said of his autobiography when he was told that something he said didn't really happen that way, "It's my memoirs and that's the way I remember it." Also a famous author said of a book he wrote, "I wrote it as fiction mainly because it can be more true as fiction than as history." What one knows as a fact doesn't have to be proved, but can be included as the author believes they are true.

I am writing this story because I feel I had a wonderful opportunity to live through a unique experience during World War II—land combat, being bombed, strafed from the air, bombarded from the sea, experiencing an invasion from the sea, repelling a sea invasion, and finally being captured by the enemy and brutalized both mentally and physically. I was also privileged to see the enemy military as it lived, worked, and fought from the civilian aspect of war-time Japan, to the final closing, and being within 30 miles of Nagasaki and the bomb itself.

I was also privileged to see the war end and to move out of Japan, returning happily home to a grateful nation and a happy family.

My intent is to impart to those who read this book that it was a terrible ordeal for me and my friends and comrades, and there was an extreme loss of life.

For myself, because I survived, I want to have my readers realize I thought I was embarking on a great adventure when I left San Francisco. When the end of the great war came, I felt I had been part of a fantastic undertaking and was privileged beyond my wildest dreams to have been part of the history of World War II and American history itself.

I am not a writer; I am not an author; I am a survivor. Let my story begin.

Chapter One

OLD FORT PRESIDIO OF SAN FRANCISCO, CALIFORNIA

I was in old Fort Presidio, the home of the 30th Infantry and the headquarters for the 4th Army. This was an old Army fort in San Francisco at the south end of the Golden Gate Bridge. It was late summer 1941. The 30th Infantry was known as San Francisco's own. When they were not training elsewhere, they would parade most every morning. The band would start the march music and the 30th would pass in review, flags fluttering in the breeze, and march proudly past the reviewing stand. This was the summer before America became involved directly in World War II. We were under the 4th Army. I was with the U.S. Army Air Corps assigned to Hamilton Field, California, attending cooks and bakers school at the Presidio.

The 4th Army headquarters received word that they were to go on maneuvers and repel a Japanese Army that had hypothetically invaded Washington State. As I was in school at the time at the Presidio, I was pulled into the maneuvers. The 4th Army moved out in what I understood to be a seventy-mile-long convoy. We proceeded north as quickly as possible. We camped each night as we moved forward. The army operated like a great circus. As the convoy would be pulling into their campground for the night, others would

11

already be preparing for the next day. Many would work all night. Food service people would serve the evening meal, clean up, and start preparing for the next day. The cooks started preparing breakfast and lunch at 2:00 a.m. At first light, the convoy would be on the move again.

I was thrilled by our 15th Infantry. They came racing up beside us and our trucks left enough room in between so that every other infantry truck could swing in and out of line as they raced through our unit at high speed. I thought how I would like to be in that sharp outfit. It was wonderful and the whole trip was a thrilling experience.

I had just returned to California and to Hamilton Field when I was transferred to an Air Corps outfit leaving for overseas. I was in the outfit about ten days before we sailed. Everything had to be marked "Plum," which was a destination code. No one knew where we were going and if we got even a hint, we were not to say anything to anyone. The joke around the unit was "Right, PLUM TO HELL." We went to Angel Island in the middle of San Francisco bay where we received shots and equipment. Each man had to be carrying an Army overcoat when he walked up the gang plank. Anyone with a fever or infection of any kind was to step out of the line and would be left behind. The boat we boarded moved us across San Francisco Bay to old Fort Mason, in San Francisco on the south side of the bay. Waiting for us was a lovely liner, an around-the-world cruise ship, the *S.S. President Coolidge* with all the sound and appearance of a great liner ready to move out to sea. We were leaving a peaceful, secure, and orderly world to enter a world of excitement, mystery, adventure, terror, and death, and in the end would return with victory, exaltation, and unbelievable joy and happiness. On this day, the curtain was going up for us, not to come down for four long years.

Chapter Two

THE TRIP TO THE PHILIPPINES

I want to begin with the time we were leaving for the Philippines. I had joined in with the 34th Pursuit Squadron and our planes were on their way to the Philippines. This was in November 1941, just prior to the outbreak of the war on the 8th of December in the Orient. We loaded on a beautiful November morning, on board the *S.S. President Coolidge* with all of our supplies and equipment. We walked up the gang plank of this beautiful, chartered Presidential Line ship excited and elated, nervous with anticipation. As the ship slowly began to pull out of beautiful San Francisco harbor and pass under the Golden Gate Bridge, bells rang for lunch. We went below and saw plush rugs and an orchestra playing in the dining hall, a true picture of the old, beautiful Presidential Lines as they sailed those days in all the glories of the old Presidential Lines tour ships. We slowly slipped under the Golden Gate bridge and out into the wide Pacific to an adventure. I was excited, thrilled and nervous. I was going on a quest, but had no idea as to the deep implications that were involved, the ramifications, difficulties, excitements, and strange unexpected things I was to see.

On the beautiful *President Coolidge*, they had a promenade deck where I was to sleep. We had bunks that were four high, double on the outside and the inside. There was a row up the outside and another up the inside. In other words, I had a

25-HAMI

bunk mate beside me and bunks were four high. I was the third level, which looked directly into the continental lounge. There were great beautiful divans, easy chairs and floor lights, all in one great enormous beautiful lounge.

I was almost seasick on this trip to Hawaii. It was the first time I 'd been on the ocean and I was a little queasy. It was very nice and I enjoyed the roll of the ocean and white caps in the distance. The smell of the ocean had always been exciting to me, and now I was realizing its reality.

We arrived in Hawaii in approximately five days. I believe it was the 5th or the 6th of November that we arrived in Honolulu. We pulled slowly into the docks and oh, it was a beautiful place. It smelled like one enormous flower garden. As is in the movies and pictures you've seen, they had the beautiful girls with their leis who said, "Aloha", while putting the leis around our necks as we headed off for a day in Honolulu. Meanwhile, the ship took on various kinds of supplies and unloaded equipment that was being delivered to Hawaii. I spent a marvelous, exotic day in Honolulu. We wandered down the wide, flower-scented boulevards, out to Waikiki beach, to a little snack bar where I enjoyed a chocolate malt. I had dreamed of someday seeing this beautiful place called Hawaii, and here I was, a dream come true.

While spending the day in Hawaii, I decided to get my hair cut. I went into a barber shop and the barber who cut my hair was a bare-footed Japanese girl. She said to me, "Where are you going?" and I said, "To the Orient." When she asked, "Why?" I answered, "To fight the Japanese." She replied, "Don't say that." I clearly remember the day and the conversation, after fifty years. I was reading one of my letters to my mother, telling her about it. It surprised me, how exactly I remembered the story I had written to my mother so long ago.

The day quickly drew to an end and we gathered back at our ships at supper time and went below. Shortly after we were all on board, the ship began to clear the harbor and we pulled out towards the Far East.

As we left Honolulu, we were accompanied by the *S.S. President Grant* and a cruiser escort. As we sailed towards the Philippines, we enjoyed this time on the ship. There were 2,700 men. We had all kinds of card games on deck and many things to do. Everyone was enjoying it. But over it all hung a tense feeling, that something might really happen. The news said that the Japanese were in the United States talking about the possible settlement of a very serious situation that theoretically existed between us and the Japanese. We were told one evening to be very careful at night, don't throw any cigarettes overboard, no lights on deck, and don't throw any trash overboard. Actually, we were traveling under war-time conditions. The tenseness began to gradually increase as we were given more information. One day as I was watching a card game, idly watching the cruiser sailing several miles out to our right and just forward, I noticed all kinds of activity on the cruiser. The war ship did a swift left turn and her guns began rolling around on their turrets as she tore across our bow at top speed. All these things added to the tension, with the knowledge that something serious was in the wind.

After we had been out several nights, I was lying in my bunk whiling away my time when they called a conference of officers in the continental lounge. An officer got up to speak. He had a large chart on the black board he was using, and closed the door and said, "We want to tell you something of what you're really going into. The situation in the Philippines is that war is coming." He drew a map of the islands and said, "This is a picture of the Philippine Islands. The Japanese will attack probably in three places. One place definitely is Lingayn Gulf, probably a major attack on the opposite side of Manila, then lower Manila, in all probability

15

a three-pronged attack towards Manila. At this time, our plan is that all surviving forces will withdraw into Bataan." This was a tremendous shock to me because he didn't say "maybe," he didn't say "I think so," he said, "This will happen" to us. It totally shocked me. I almost fell out of my bunk. It was probably the 15th of November.

Chapter Three

MANILA BEFORE THE STORM

We arrived uneventfully in Manila on I believe the 20th of November. We pulled slowly into the docks and oh, what a beautiful old city. It was everything I'd ever dreamed of. I saw the park with the palm trees, the little carts that the calisa ponies pulled, and people coming down to the ship. The ship would be going back; we were all unloading and people were there to meet us with transportation. Oh, it was so exciting to me. We were given transportation to Nichols Field outside of Manila. We arrived at Nichols Field where we were put up in a tent area. Our squadron was assigned a dining area where we were to set up our own kitchens. We were next to some elegant old barracks. As I recall, they were wooden with handsome big screen porches. I enjoyed the few days we were there and going to the little snack bars. We ate in their dining halls when we first arrived and nearby were these beautiful, old cool wooden barracks with their enormous screen porches. We had the barbers in our area where we paid a monthly fee of $3.00 to have our barber work done. We could go to the barber shop whenever we wanted. It was great. It was relaxed. It was idyllic. It was an example of a dream, the relaxed atmosphere the people lived in, but it didn't last long.

A night or two after we arrived, all the whistles began blowing, and everybody was running all over and dragging guns and vehicles were tearing around. I said, "What in the world is going on?" and they said, "It's a red alert. We're on alert status here and we fall out every few nights and go through a full practice." I said, "Oh, for goodness sake." I could hardly believe all this was going on. But, we set up anyway and did have some wonderful times during this period.

We arrived approximately November 20th, then went out to Del Carmen about the 29th, so I'm talking about a short nine days. In those nine days, I went to Manila almost every night. The routine work knocked off at 1:00 p.m. so those who didn't have a specific duty would go to town. We would dress up in shark-skin (silk) clothes and tropical gear and off we'd go to Manila. Manila was exciting. It was full of the sounds of the day. The United States was the country and the Philippines were part of our territory, and the people were living a happy, quiet, relaxed life, the best I could tell. It was all so beautiful. We visited places in town, rode in the old carts, went out and visited the University of Philippines, around to various bars and little restaurants the people frequented. I thought Manila was absolutely gorgeous. There were landscaped, tree-lined streets, rivers, the ocean, and the classic old Spanish walled city. We also visited the Manila Hotel, a landmark for the people in the Philippines. I had a wonderful time in Manila those nine days. Every minute I wasn't working, I was there.

All this was to come to a swift conclusion on Saturday, which I believe was the 29th of November. I have read that the Japanese were putting on the purple machine, or the code which we had cracked at that time, that irrevocable military action would commence on the 29th of November. As we had broken their code without their knowledge, we were aware of their plans. According to information I have read, the American government had already heard them say that they were committed to war as of approximately October 7 and all their actions were leading up to war. This was unknown to the general public, and it's quite obvious why they couldn't be told, because we knew what was going on. If we told the people that we knew, the Japanese would know we knew. If the Japanese found out, they would change their plans and we would certainly have been caught much more unaware than we were.

All this led to the actual beginning of World War II and the attack on the Philippines as I observed it. On November 29th, a new era of excitement spread through the camp. We were told we were going to leave Manila in a hurry. In fact, we had to leave that afternoon, as soon as we were able to get our equipment on the trucks. We were asked what we would like to carry. At this time, being an impressionable young man, I was curious about all the excitement. I asked my first sergeant, "What's going on anyway?" He said, "Well, some of us think the war has already started." We didn't know what this meant. It was a mystery to me. What in the world was happening? By late afternoon, nearing dark, we got our equipment on the trucks, and as we pulled away from Nichols Field, we passed by the officers' club. I remember seeing officers in their beautiful white suits standing around on the patio, where they were having a party. The general color, the festivities, the good times the Philippines represented, including the soft sounds of dance music, have never left my memory.

Chapter Four

DEL CARMEN FIELD

We were abandoning Manila at high speed. Our trucks drove all night. The next morning we arrived at Del Carmen Field. A sugar cane field had been cleared for our airplanes. Tents had been set up for us. We moved in and began to prepare for a new life, whatever it was. Nearby was another tent group, the 803rd Engineers. Tents and kitchen tents were set up. It was a beautiful, interesting atmosphere. Off to the side, a short distance to our west, was the Zambalies Mountains. As we would learn later, they divided us from the flatlands we were living on. Where the ground rose into the Zambalies, there was a beautiful little clear river where we went for our bathing and swimming and relaxation from time to time. It was fun in a way, and I enjoyed it. It was almost like camping out. Down in the Zambalies, we had our washing place and a little grass-type shelter that had been built by someone. It had poles around the outside, a roof of grass, and was shaded underneath, a very nice place with a park-type atmosphere. I remember taking some food and having our lunches by the river. It was nice, but this was all a short duration. We only got hints here and there such as the first sergeant saying he thought the war had already started. The Filipino people asked, "Do you think the Japanese will really make war?" We said, "Oh no, not really. They're too smart for that. They wouldn't take a chance on attacking us." But time was

20

moving swiftly, and within a few days our commander, Lt. Merritt, came back from Clark Field. He called us together and said there's going to be war within 72 hours. He said, "I've just been advised of this at a top level briefing at Clark Field. Let's all get out there and dig holes, set up our weapons, and maybe half of us will go home." That was an astounding statement to us, incredulous. Everybody listened, everybody dug, yet no one believed, not really. No, it's just maybe, just scare talk.

On Sunday night we went to town. The small group I was with rented a taxi cab and saw the city of Angeles. We spent a considerable part of the evening visiting bars and as soldiers habits are, drinking a Coke and having a little of this and a little of that. You always want to have a snack and of course, the drinkers want to drink. As I'm a Coke drinker, I always had my Coke. We had a very pleasant evening in Angeles and in the wee hours of the morning, we went back in a cab. Th cab was very cheap; I think it was $3.00 between us. There were four of us in the cab and we kicked in something like 75 cents each. Really an incredible thing for now, even incredible for then, to get a taxi cab. Our camp was probably 15 miles from Angeles. We got in bed early in the morning, as it was just beginning to get light. My bed was an old canvas-type, an Army cot.

Morning began to break, a cool summer morning. In the Philippines, it's summer year round. We didn't ever really have any cold weather in the Philippines. The smell and sounds of morning were coming in as daylight began to appear. You'd hear little noises of the camp, radios, and then people running up and down the street. We got up to see what in the world was going on because the radio seemed to be running loud and everybody was hurrying around to see what was up. We went over to one of the radios and there was an announcement that Pearl Harbor had been attacked. Smoke was rising from Pearl Harbor;

they had been attacked by Japanese airplanes. We were really under attack by the Japanese. Even though we had been told approximately 72 hours prior to this, it was still very shocking. Nobody believed it. Nobody expected it. Suddenly it was thrust on us. There it was. Everyone stood around in little clusters and talked about it and thought about it and made such comments as, "I wonder how long it will last? Thirty days? Well, at least we'll get to go home sooner, because this war surely won't last long."

We possessed total confidence in American power and total contempt for the Japanese and their capabilities. We were led to believe they had a very inadequate air force and their pilots had bad eyesight. We were to learn later that these things were totally erroneous. One of the training programs for Japanese pilots was to locate certain stars in the daytime, a trick that, to me, seemed impossible. The few times I made any attempt to try were totally fruitless. But still, they did say that Japanese pilots were trained to identify stars in the daytime. That's just unbelievable to me. In any case, we had a totally erroneous idea of the capabilities and power of the Japanese Air Force and Army, and their determination.

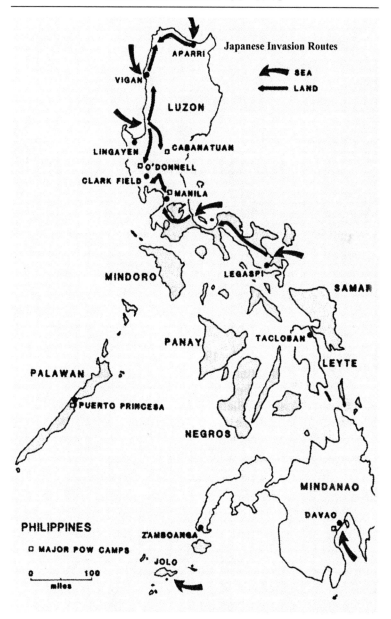

Japanese landing in Philippine Islands between 8 - 20
December 1941

25-HAMI

Chapter Five

THE JAPANESE ARE HERE

We had a little breakfast and went down to the river to wash and shave to start the new day. Even though they had attacked Pearl Harbor, Hawaii, we were much closer to Formosa. The morning wore on and people began to get used to the idea. About 11 o'clock, we saw a couple of Japanese planes scooting along pretty high up. As far as we could tell, just staying out of the way of our planes which reinforced the idea that we're seeing a little action but they're not really going to give us a rough time.

At noon the radio was on from Clark Field, I was standing around the radio shack and we got a call that our outfit, the 34th Pursuit Squadron, should put some planes up because Clark Field was coming under attack. Clark Field was in sight, but quite some distance away. To see planes overhead was pretty difficult. Our pilots immediately began taking off. The dust was blowing, the planes were roaring and oh, the excitement of everybody getting airborne and rushing around. We were still confident of our capabilities, our own people and confident everything would be satisfactory. What actually did occur are some of the things I heard later in the day and read in history books in later years. Certainly, I heard about it that night. People at Clark during the actual attack were back at our place and I was able to talk to some of them, who were eating in the dining halls at the time. What happened was that shortly after 12, probably 12:25, it came over the radio in the dining halls that Clark Field was under attack. Some people who were eating lunch went outside and looked. Some looked out the windows and there was a general scoffing and laughing. Everybody's all mixed up, as usual. Then, 54 bombers, silver in color and traveling in a beautiful formation, began approaching the field from the north. They were followed by 34 Zeroes (fighter planes). As people began to hear the sounds of the bombers, the diners rushed outside the dining halls to look at this beautiful formation of planes approaching Clark Field. Many people were still of the opinion they were American planes and that help had arrived. The total impact of what was happening, what was going to happen, what we were seeing here, had not gotten through at all. Within a few minutes, the bombs began dropping and everything became total chaos: bombs everywhere, dust flying, airplanes being blown to pieces, people being hit, and dining halls being hit, but the main attack was on the runway. Our planes had been flying around all morning trying to get orders on what exactly they were doing. They were as confused as the men on the ground and near noon they were advised to come back, land, have lunch, refuel and see what was going to happen. Most of the planes were on the ground. Pilots ran for their planes in an attempt to get back in the air. They had little success, but a few did get up and there were a few exciting stories, but that's another story, another book. That's not my story because I wasn't flying. My story is what I saw and what I know happened.

After the day had closed, we were at Del Carmen. The people who had been at Clark came in dusty and dirty, telling their story. There was tremendous excitement around camp. It was beginning to sink in. This was really war. We're really in a war and we're not going to win it the first day. We'd taken a lot of casualties. We lost a lot of airplanes. It isn't the good-time party everybody thought it was going to be. It's going to be a real war. As the night wore on, people talked, worried, became concerned and began to assimilate what was happening. We bedded down for a new day.

In the morning, dawn found us in a war. We were attacked again. Planes were attacking other places in the Philippines and as they came through our area, they would strafe anything they saw. In the meantime, we pulled our tents down, moved in among the rocks to where we could be more or less hidden, and placed our cook tent under an enormous tree. It was a beautiful old tree. It had great wide roots and one of these open type grid affairs where you could walk in one side of the tree and out the other, an enormous tree. I was a young man at the time and memory is not what it used to be, but at this time, as I recall, it was a fantastic tree – – – tall and beautiful with big shade. Suffice to say, we were able to set our kitchen up under this tree, where it couldn't be seen from the air. Some Filipinos who were with us said there was an enormous python that lived in the tree. This made us kind of edgy and the tree became more mysterious and exciting. We set our sleeping areas up around it. I was a cook, so naturally the cooks were near the cook tent. We were nervous about all the snakes. In our position under this great, enormous tree, we were able to look out across the flying field where our planes landed.

On either the second or third day, we came under attack by strafing planes. There were either five or six airplanes. They flew in great enormous circles over our field. This was one of the most terrifying, hair raising feelings I had experienced up to this time. These planes were making great circles with the whining of the engines as they pulled around in a long circle, getting a good view of what they intended to do. We know that the circle meant something disastrous was about to happen; it was a tense, exciting moment. As they completed the full circle, they began their dive. The planes came down in a long screaming plunge towards the runway. As they passed over, their airplanes had a gun in front that was firing and tearing away at our parked airplanes. A gun in the back was swinging around, too. They had a rotating gun. In fact, you could see them quite plainly from the ground as they made their low level pass over the runway, with this man in the back working this machine gun on any object that looked likely to him. We were quite concerned, scared in fact, that he might spot us under our tree. He did spot a big pile of Army blue barracks bags down at the end of the runway. I'm sure he thought they were troops in Army fatigues because we wore fatigues of this color, the same as those bags. They made a fast pass and fired on these bags continually, feeling, I am sure, that they had found all of the personnel and killed them. In this particular case, we lost our airplanes but we hadn't lost our men. No personnel were killed in the attack. It was purely an equipment loss as far as we were concerned. By the time these strafers finished, our planes were a total wreck. We were through as an effective Air Force unit. At this time, our senior officer was a Lt. Brown.

Our squadron had flown out that morning and at the same time there was a major Japanese landing at Aparri, to the north of where we were. It was on the northern tip of Luzon. Our fighter squadron had passed over some of their ships and attacked a large vessel. As our squadron commander passed over this ship, firing into it, at that exact moment the ship had a tremendous explosion and caught Lt. Merritt's plane in the blast. His plane was torn to pieces and he was lost. So, when our squadron returned for lunch that day, just prior to the strafing attack, it was a sad occasion because they had to tell us our commander had been killed and would not be returning.

After the strafing attack, we were advised Lt. Brown was now our commander, we had no airplanes, and we would be leaving as soon as possible. As there were no airplanes and nothing to do, the decision was to go to Del Carmen, a town. Shortly after lunch we all proceeded to Del Carmen, a small sugar central town nearby. In Del Carmen, there was a place where you could send messages and all of us that could, probably everybody, went there to send a Western Union message back home. It was the first time we had a chance to tell our families back home where we were and that we're in the war. When we first shipped out to the Philippines, of course we shipped out under orders, unable to tell anybody where we were going, because we didn't know anyway. We were told after we got to the Philippines not to write our family and tell them where we were. So, being a very dutiful young man at the time, and very conscientious, I had not written my folks. But now we could send a message home and say that we were in a war. I think one of our old sergeants sent a message that said, "Bombed and strafed, scared and safe." That's about all he could send, something of that nature. I don't even remember what I sent off and I don't know if the message ever got through. There was an air of excitement that night at Del Carmen. The war was on. We had lost our airplanes. We moved into this little barrio. It had an American bar, Filipino bar and a bakery which our own people were operating. It was decided as evening wore on that it wouldn't be safe any place in town, so we would move out to the golf course. We took all of our sleeping equipment and moved out there to spend the night. We bedded down on the putting green, very tense and excited. Sometime in the evening, I suppose 10 or 11 o'clock, an airplane flew over and dropped a flare. Nobody knew, and probably nobody knows to this day, what that was about, but it caused some pretty heavy panic because we could visualize almost anything – —such as the enemy knowing where we were and spotting us with a flare to make some kind of an attack on us. I'm sure it wasn't anything nearly that insidious. I'm sure some poor pilot was lost and trying to find out where he was, but imagine the frantic feelings that night when the flare went off and people got up and ran. A couple of guys fell over a cliff because of the excitement, but were not really hurt. Everybody was like a bunch of nervous horses. We were easy to spook. This will give you some idea what it was like, what was going on, the early moments, the early days of the war. This was how it was for an impressionable young man fresh off the farm.

We stayed in Del Carmen for a few days and I remember quite vividly that there were all kinds of flashing lights at night which appeared to be signals. We did some firing at some of the lights. We advised all the inhabitants no signaling, no blinking lights, but it seemed the lights were blinking everywhere. I presume we were involved with sympathizers —people who were with the Japanese. Of course, you never really knew. We only knew there was a fantastic amount of blinking lights. A few days after this, we returned to Del Carmen Field where we set up and operated an emergency-type landing strip for anything that might be needed. We came under many attacks in the few days as we maintained our strip at Del Carmen Field. They were exciting, they were scary, they were something really unique, especially to a young man like myself who had seen so little. The descriptive nature of what it is like to come under an actual bombing attack is that it is a very frightening experience. It's a tremendous feeling, hard to transmit, about how it really is. We would see the bombers coming, and as they approached overhead, we could tell they were on line and were most certainly going to bomb us. They knew we were there. There was almost no choice so the question was, "Where will they bomb?" We quickly learned where the bad spots were. If they passed a certain area, we knew they were going to pass us by. If they started bombing early enough, we didn't have to worry too much because they'd run out of bombs before they got to us.

If we were in fact going to be bombed in our area, we crouched down in our holes with a feeling of, "Wow, we just can't get away from it." As you bury your head and lay low to escape the flying shrapnel you know is going to occur, naturally you're not going to look up to see the bombs fall. If you do, it's more dangerous, and in the second place, it's kind of like getting your tooth pulled: you don't want to look anyway. As you lay there and hold your head close to the ground, you hear the tremendous "thud, thud, crash, thud" as bombs hit and explode. As they come—one, two, three— each blast feels as if some enormous giant is walking up on you. The earth shakes with each step; it's a tremendously exciting and terrifying experience. I never knew whether they're going to run out before they got to me, or whether they were going to pass over, or, in fact, if I was going to be hit. A bombing experience is like no other experience of war. They're sometimes unbelievable in their terror. The immensity of the emotional feeling that flows over you is almost beyond description. For a young man, it's similar to the terrible risks taken on motorcycles, both terrorizing and exciting.

As I think back on the things that happened at Del Carmen field and of the short period of time I was there, it rather astounds me that so much happened. At one point we were in this round, shelter-type place down by the Zambalies during those weeks after the attack, until we abandoned the place the day before Christmas. We spent a considerable amount of time on the river bank. One evening we were having coffee. We got jelly and jams in big #10 tin cans, about a gallon or so. Six or eight of us were having a little coffee and some jam one night, when all of a sudden, we realized we were totally surrounded. We were looking up at 20 to 30 midgets, Igarottes (natives), standing in a circle around us, dressed only in G-strings with weapons tied to their sides. They were little men who looked like children with beards. It was unbelievable to suddenly look up and see you're totally surrounded by small people carrying spears and little bows and arrows and knives. It was a frightening experience; on the other hand, very interesting to look up and see you're hemmed in by pygmies. They were very friendly and we offered them some bread and jam. They all participated and there was a lot of laughing and carrying on—what a colorful side note to the war. The Igarottes lived just the other side of the river, up in the hills. We walked up there a few times and saw them living in the most primitive tepee-type huts. You would see women carrying babies who looked like tiny children themselves. It was an unbelievable experience.

We approached Christmas time and the bombings went on. We received many messages about how the war was progressing. We knew the Japanese had landed in the north. We lost all of our planes. There weren't many planes left in the Philippines but if we did receive any planes, we'd have a place for them. If any emergency landings were necessary, we were there.

Just prior to Christmas day, we moved to Del Carmen again. Del Carmen was the same place we had been for the few nights when we slept on the golf course. They had an American club there and it was a nice place. It was set up with a nice kitchen and dining room very similar to a country club building. There was a bowling alley, swimming pool, and green grass. It was very pretty. We stayed there several nights. I don't recall exactly how many, but we had Christmas dinner there. We set Christmas dinner up just like we would have at home. We used china plates from the club. We cooked

Christmas dinner in the stove. We used real silverware. They had a library with books on the bookshelves on the wall. In other words, we were living in an American atmosphere for the very last time for three and a half years. It was beautiful, relaxed, and yet in the middle of a dying lifestyle and dying people. Unreal, to say the least.

A jeep came through on Christmas day and an American captain stopped to talk to us a few minutes. He was coming from the front and we asked him how everything was going. Knowing we had been listening to radio Manila and they were saying we were holding on all fronts, the captain told us, "Holding on all fronts in this case means we're retreating as fast as they're advancing." In other words, we were making a successful withdrawal. This was a shocking and depressing announcement. Even though we had lost our own airplanes, even though we were in a real war, it still hadn't gotten through to us that it was a losing war. All of this was beginning to come clear very gradually.

As we sat in the club at Del Carmen, we could see the bombers passing over to bomb Clark Field and could hear the explosions at Clark Field. We learned later that Clark Field was being abandoned and many of the explosions we heard were being set by our own people, leaving nothing to be captured by the Japanese.

Christmas day ended. A beautiful day. A real Christmas dinner. An all-American day. The sun went down, it got dark and night came. I and Quintan Kulman, another cook, made our bed out in the yard and when we woke up in the morning, we found everybody had gone but us. We were the only two left. They had not wakened us because they had left us with Sgt. Godby, the mess sergeant, to close up and bring whatever was left. It was a frightening experience to wake up in the morning and find everybody gone, and we were the ones who were going to bring what was left, and we were actually retreating. It wasn't long before we packed up what we needed and the truck came to pick us up. We hurried on to Orani, which is in the mouth of the peninsula into Bataan. It is the only road on the west side, the only clear and easy way to drive to Bataan. Since everybody was retreating, the entire American Army was going to come down this road. Even the advancing Japanese Army was going to come down this road and was naturally going to come under air attack, under all sorts of attack. We sat up outside a school house outside of Orani, just to the north as you entered the town, so the town and the escape route lay south of us. To the north lay the clear road of our retreating Army. The Army, civilians, everyone who was fleeing from the Japanese Army was using this road.

This road was jammed with trucks, carts, cars, people, women and children, soldiers in vehicles, guns being towed, food trucks, all types of supplies, everything. The road was jammed. As we looked to the north at the clear, flat, straight road, every so often a Japanese plane or two would pass over, strafing the people on the road. Everybody would scatter, jump in the ditches and lay down. After the strafing swept over them, they ran back to their vehicles and took off again in a mad rush to escape. Planes were roaring around all over, particularly Japanese planes. We still had a few P-40 fighter planes available and some were in the action. I remember looking out over this summer-like afternoon at the panorama of struggle and excitement going down the road. I saw one of our fighter planes approach a group of three Japanese planes that were busily bombing, and they strafed the Japanese planes as they were bombing. I noticed an anti-aircraft gun firing away. It hit one of the Japanese planes and it went down in a pillar of smoke. This was all part of the crushing scenario going on before my eyes, like a wide-screen movie. This excitement and milling went on for several days.

One afternoon, the town's bridge came under a tremendous attack from bombers. People were hanging around a church near the bridge. There were cock fights, people hiding out, refugees who didn't know where they were going or how far they were going or what to do, and townspeople. When the bombers struck, there were all kinds of casualties. Trucks roared up the road bringing the wounded to the school house where we were. We were outside the school house with our field kitchens. We were boiling water as fast as we could for the doctors and the nurses and the people that were there to try to help the wounded. The trucks rushed in with the wounded women, children, and men, and the badly hurt were unloaded. The planes were screaming overhead. It was a tremendous scene. We took a couple of bombs in our area. It hit some small buildings we had there. It all added to the confusion, the melee and the excitement of the moment. Someone came by and said they needed more doctors. They wanted someone to go forward to the front to see if there were any doctors available for all of the casualties we had taken. I had had enough of the confusion and the excitement and would do anything to get out of it. so I volunteered to go forward. I got in a vehicle with another soldier and we rushed off to the front to see if we could rustle up a doctor. We got there and it was worse than at our school house. They were under heavy attack. There was heavy artillery fire. There were airplanes. Everybody was in and out of their holes so fast you couldn't talk to anybody. Nobody had any time for anything. We soon discovered that any attempt to get any doctors away from the front was useless, so we returned to our area.

The front was rapidly approaching. We were in a fixed position, an exciting and dangerous position to occupy, a terrifying position to occupy. That night as I lay on my cot, I heard the roll and roar of artillery at the front. Every time we'd hear another roll of artillery, it would sound closer. It got closer and louder and closer and louder. Each exchange seemed much closer. This was extenuated by the fact we were defending with retreating tanks. They, the enemy, were bringing up tanks and artillery as fast as we abandoned each position. Each salvo and heavy exchange of fire would sound closer. I was upset and nervous by this time. By morning, the decision had been made that our group would make another movement to the rear because we were Air Force and not actually combat soldiers. The actual frontline combat was being carried on by the 192nd Tank, 194th Tank, 31st Infantry, Filipino scouts, Filipino Army, and other scattered units that had been drawn in as extra infantry. We were still considered Air Force and not infantry.

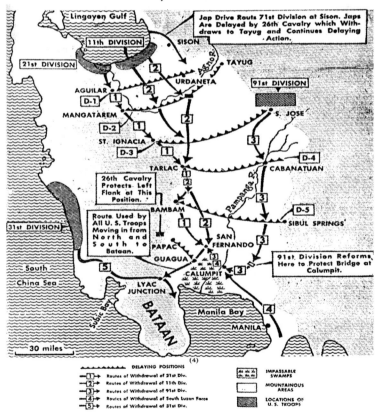

Japanese advance from Lingayen Gulf to Bataan

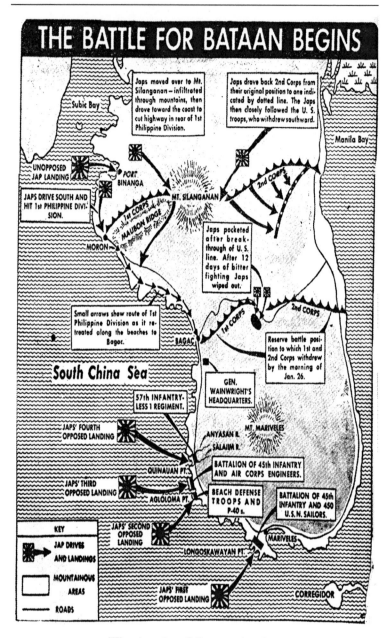

The battle of Bataan begins

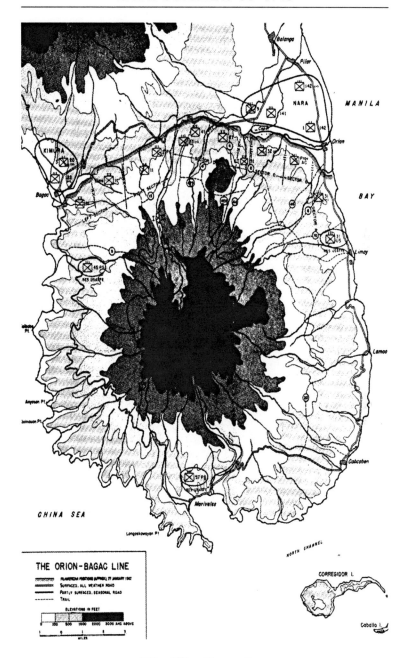

The Pilar Bagac line

37

Chapter Six

THE WITHDRAWAL INTO BATAAN

We retreated to the Bataan Peninsula, directly across from Corregidor. The number one hospital was across the road from us and we were below the hospital on the southeast side of the road as the mountains slope down towards the bay. We could look directly out on Corregidor. That morning as we prepared the noon meal. I assume it was lunch because we left early in the morning we were in these beautiful woods. There was a new feeling. No firing could be heard. A feeling was that maybe we had reached some kind of sanctuary or maybe we were far enough in the rear where we'd be all right. All that was shattered very quickly. Someone had hooked up a radio and a broadcast came from radio Manila. "The remnants of MacArthur's forces have now retreated into Bataan and are in hiding in the woods directly across from Corregidor." This was an unnerving announcement because that was the exact position we were sitting in. How many were with us was hard to know, but certainly I knew where they thought a good group of us were. This was basically semantics because the main percentage of the Army was withdrawing grudgingly down the peninsula and fighting an effective and efficient battle. We did very well, particularly because we had a narrow area to defend. We had good defensive positions, and even though we were short of ammunition and equipment, we were able to take up many effective positions. The Japanese had to push slowly, directly into our fortified guns, a bad position for any army to be in. We were able to retreat down the peninsula, but because there were overwhelming numbers pursuing our Army, it couldn't work out successfully in the end.

We were in the jungles across from the hospital. We stayed there a few days and then were told we were going to move. We loaded our equipment in our trucks and we went to kilometer 191, Agaloma Bay. We arrived in the dark and went down a long winding road. It was a beautiful moonlit night. We'd break out of the trees occasionally and could see the China Sea. It was a beautiful sight. We stopped for a bit to get our bearings and have a little supper. We warmed some coffee and opened a few cans of fruit and so forth, just a little supper before we continued on. One of the guys said looking out at this dense jungle, "I bet there's snakes out there that haven't bit anybody 'cause there isn't anyone to bite."

We moved on into a nice open space, lined by trees, where we set up a permanent camp. We were in this camp for approximately two weeks in very pleasant conditions. We had a nice camp with huge shade trees. We had more or less a permanent area. Our duty was to guard the beaches, so we spread our people out and waited. Being a cook, I had to be close to the camp. We enjoyed gorgeous moonlit nights under these great tall tropical trees. Five or six fellows in the outfit had guitars or stringed instruments, and there were also some beautiful singers. First Sgt. Hugely had a fantastic voice. At night we would sit in the jungle, drink coffee and some of the men would play music. It was a beautiful interlude, a picnic, camp out, almost like a Boy Scout camp. I could write a whole book, I suppose, on this two week camp out. We had food from Manila. We sent out scouting parties to look for supplies. It was a beautiful little camp and the circumstances, unreal.

Chapter Seven

THE BATTLE OF AGALOMA BAY

One night after almost two weeks, I felt rather apprehensive and went up to the radio shack to listen to the radio. I heard somebody at Gway Bay on the radio say, "I saw a light. Did anybody see a light?" That made me nervous. They said they had not, so I went back to my bunk, got my rifle out handy, my shoes where I could find them, my ammunition where I could find it, and went to bed. At about 3 o'clock in the morning we were suddenly awakened and told to get up and get dressed, because there had been a landing on our beach. Nervous and alert, in a few minutes I was ready to go. What had happened was about 1 o'clock in the morning, a young man in our outfit named Rabbit was at the point and watching out across the China Sea. He saw something, called the CP and told them that he had seen some boats. An officer went down, looked and didn't see anything. They told Rabbit to go to bed and forget it. A little bit before 3 A.M., Sgt. Jones of our outfit was on the point at Agaloma Bay. He called on the phone and said, "Five boats were approaching my position." He asked for permission to fire. They couldn't find anybody to give him permission because they didn't know what the boats were. There were always a certain number of boats moving up and down the coast at night so they didn't want to fire on friendly boats. Within a few minutes, the boats began scraping sand and Jones started to fire. He fired four rounds with his 30 caliber machine gun and it jammed. He had an air cooled 30 caliber which he grabbed and fired, holding it with his bare hands. He fired until the barrel got so hot it burnt his hands something terrible. In the meantime, all the Japanese got out of the boats and scrambled up the cliffs. All was quiet and he didn't know what was going on. He abandoned his gun, rolled off the cliff and ran down the beach towards camp and got away.

We were all called to the beach. We got out of our trucks and worked our way down towards the edge of the water. In the meantime, a young fellow was killed. As far as I know, he was the first man killed in our organization on Bataan. He had been a cook and he wanted to be a scout. He had taken some ROTC in high school and was very eager to be a real military man. He wanted to be a scout and they had decided to let him. He went to where Jones had abandoned his gun. He slipped up the trail very quietly, watching for anything, and walked up to where Jones had his phone. He picked up the phone, called the CP and said, "There's nobody here." At just about that time a rifle shot rang out and he fell. It was discovered later that anywhere between 500 and 700 men were in this area comprising only a few acres. They had to be in there thick and deep. Because of our position and because of the denseness of the jungle, some unbelievable things happened, such as this young man getting to the phone in the first place. In the second place, two people went out to pick him up. They found him, picked him up on a stretcher, and carried him back down the trail without being shot themselves. This is almost unbelievable. I have no idea how this occurred – —whether the Japanese were busy with something else, or whether they didn't want to give their position away, or what.

The Japanese had gotten ashore. We have arrived on the beach. We have lost one man and he has been carried successfully out. There is no way to know the strength of the forces we are facing or what condition they are in. We are in a strange situation. It is barely dawn and as I stood on this beach at Agaloma Bay at the top of the Agaloma River, I have a bad feeling about what is going to happen next. Everything is quiet. We have in position 13 twin 50 caliber machine guns, 20 30-caliber machine guns, a 2.95 mountain gun and a 4-inch naval gun. We had an undetermined number of Japanese ashore and in position. We had in our own outfit, something like 230 people, spread out over three bays. Suddenly, in the quiet of the morning a shot rings out, a machine gun blast and then machine guns are firing everywhere, tracers are crossing the sky absolute bedlam. Apprehension was replaced by intense excitement and tremendous sounds of battle. We are in a brand new situation, a brand new place, and a brand new battle since we left our last battle at Del Carmen. Nothing decisive was determined at this time. The Japanese were well dug in. We in no way had enough forces to drive them out or capture or destroy them. They were busily digging in, preparing their positions, determining what they were going to do. We were beginning an unknown period of time before this situation would be resolved. These people had landed and were ashore. We took up our positions, set our machine guns and the battle field settled down where everybody's waiting and watching again. We moved our kitchens and equipment down to Agaloma River and we're only maybe a half a mile from where the Japanese are dug in. We had the Agaloma River to our backs. Our people had moved down and taken up defensive positions. The Japanese are dug in. We had no real reasonable idea of how many, but quite sure it was a sizable group. They are in dense jungle and there is absolutely no point in our present forces attempting to destroy them. Requests went out for additional help. We have been made provisional infantry. We were Air Corps. and not considered to be infantry. But for now, we have been declared provisional infantry and issued rifles and we now take up infantry duties. It was obvious we did not have the strength to control, destroy or if necessary contain the number of troops that were facing us. Some Philippine outfits were brought in, I believe the 45th Scouts. There was also another part of a Scout outfit brought in, some of the 57th. They brought several tanks up to be used later and some bren gun carriers. We set up three major machine guns close to the Japanese in addition to our fixed positions. I gathered most of this from *The Official U.S. History of the Fall of the Philippines*. It refers to this as the Battle of the Beaches in which General Homma committed an entire division to the west coast for the purpose of breaching the back side of the Bataan Peninsula. He reasoned that if the road that encircled the peninsula on the outer perimeter, which was the only really passable area of the peninsula, could be cut in several places he could divide the Army's fighting at the front. At the very least, he could disrupt the rear and possibly destroy the whole front in this manner. His movement of one entire division to the west coast in the Battle of the Beaches was a heavy commitment on his part. The official history of the Battle of the Beaches says that General Homma's official report says his division vanished without a trace. He didn't get any of his people back, but I'm sure he knew what happened to them. To say they vanished without a trace would not be a satisfactory statement. We had something like 500 to 700 people ashore in our area. There was a landing further down closer to Mariveles. A truck driver was talking to us and threw quite a scare into some of us. He said, "Here you are down on the beaches where you don't know what you're doing and they're already getting ready to cut the roads behind you. You'll be cut off completely from the back and from the rest of the forces. You'll have no way to rejoin the rest of the troops." This was a nerve racking thing for him to say and I remember it as being traumatic to a lot of the people. We moved into Agaloma River area where we set up a new kitchen. We also set up a new defensive position where we were relatively stalemated for several weeks. We received some assistance from the rear. We had artillery fire from 105s and 155s firing into the Japanese positions. The shells would pass overhead. The Japanese would be firing, too, and we would hear limbs and leaves being cut in the trees overhead. We were again in a battle situation. again on the front lines. We were listening to the rattle and roar of machine guns, the roar of cannons, the heavy artillery pieces and the Japanese moved in destroyers from the sea within firing range. The destroyers lay out far enough that our 4 inch naval gun couldn't reach them and yet their guns could reach us which added to the noise and the confusion and the general clatter of battle. On a night when the naval guns were firing from the sea, we heard a report there was a bunch of boats far out on the water. Quintan Kulman, who was standing guard, called out in a loud voice, "We're coming under fire!" Everybody jumped up from where they had been sleeping in the kitchen area, and at that very moment a shell exploded in the kitchen. It was the most deafening noise I've ever heard in my life. It felt to me as if I'd been hit in the head with a rock, with that exploding feeling where there's lights and flashes. When I was a boy, I was hit in the head by one of these hard clay things that clump along the creek bottom and are almost like a rock. My cousin threw one and hit me in the head. I got about the same feeling, lights flashing, bright spots in my eyes, a tremendous bang and then a flash of light in the kitchen. Fortunately, we had only one person hurt. Our stoves and our pots had holes in them. The shell had apparently hit in the treetop right over the kitchen and exploded as it hit the trees. Someone said, "Does anybody want to help carry this man to the hospital?" His name was Gargantis and I thought, boy, here's a chance to get out of this noise. It beats staying here. I said I would take him and we carried him on a cot. The medic Berlin and myself carried Gargantis up to the ambulance. We put him in and took him to the aid station at the old campground up on the side of the hill. We had found out that Gargantis had taken a large piece of shrapnel in his upper buttocks and lower back. I didn't know how bad he was hurt at the time, although it was a massive wound. They said to "Berlin," the medic I was with, "there's been an injury out on the point. Go out there and pick him up." Our guys were firing this 295 mountain gun out on the Point, and as they were calling range and asmith, the gun barrel kept moving. Everybody was so busy that nobody noticed that the gun was being slowly turned until it faced a tree. The gun turned until it fired point blank into the tree. There was a tremendous muzzle blast and several people were wounded. I wasn't too pleased with the idea, but on the other hand it was something to do. It was a wild night and so away we went. As we went out over the trails towards the south point of Agaloma Bay where the gun position was, we slowly climbed higher. Berlin kept calling, "Guard, guard." He said, "There's supposed to be a guard along here" but we never did find one. In the meantime, the trail rose higher and we could see all these barges coming in. It was a moonlit night. The Japanese had a system for their landings. They wanted to land just before the full moon and then just as the moon came up they would have the light to use for going ashore. This was the most dangerous time, when the moon was bright. As we traveled along these beaches, we rose higher and higher on the cliffs and we could begin to see the Japanese barges coming towards shore. There were 30 barges and their old engines were going "chung, chung, chung, chung, chung, chung." You can imagine some 30 barges out there chunging towards the beach and here we are, sitting in front of them. How many people were in those 30 barges?. I understood later there were probably 3,000 men in those 30 barges. The navel guns were firing from the sea and with our 295 gun, our naval gun, our twin 50s, and 30 caliber, we

AMI

were firing on the barges. I was looking at another tremendous panorama of battle, 30 barges approaching the beaches, the machine guns firing into the barges, the cannons firing at the barges, the naval guns firing from the sea. We were close to Corregidor and their guns began firing, too. They had 14 inch guns on Corregidor and to add to the melee, PT boats were racing around the barges out in the water. We could hardly see the PT boats but they were traveling something in the neighborhood of 60 miles per hour. They made a tremendous roar as they passed these barges, firing away. Also, several of our airplanes joined in the melee. I was at this moment, standing on a high point, say 60 feet above the water, under some trees, looking out over the water where the moon had just risen. I could see 30 barges with machine guns being fired at them, cannons being fired into them, naval guns firing from the sea, big guns firing from Corregidor, and PT boats racing around, with thunderous explosions, roars and rattles—the tremendous noise of battle. I was an abstract spectator, viewing a frightening war scene. Except for the incoming naval fire, we were taking no damaging blows, the action was all on the water. This was a time in my life when I was able to see a great battle in progress. We picked up our man that was wounded and hurried back to the hospital and I returned to my camp again. As the battle roared on, the barges were eventually all turned away. Any that made it actually landed on the beach north of us, probably 1,200 men out of 3,000 people that were in those boats that night. If the entire 3,000 had landed on our beaches as planned, I am sure I wouldn't have survived the night and certainly not the following day. Due to huge fire power, we were able to lay down from the shore, and if it wasn't for the assistance from Corregidor and the help from the PT boats, the night could have been a total disaster. As it turned out, General Homma's objective of breaking the back side of Bataan was a total failure. In fact, General Homma's official report says his division disappeared without a trace. They did land somewhere between 900 and 1,200 men that night to the north of us. They were eventually contained and totally destroyed. This was their biggest effort and it failed. Our action that night prevented the whole west coast beach operation, the Battle of the Beaches, from being a success. I saw the battle go on before my very eyes. However, we still had some 700 soldiers before us in deep jungle. After this wild night ended, we fell back into the routine of continuing our battle with the 700 Japanese in front of us. They put up a tremendous battle and it was a long, drawn out affair. We went through many exciting moments. We were bombed on occasion, and we continued to be shelled from the sea. We had three main machine gun positions close into the Japanese positions, and one night I remember quite vividly they overran our positions. Our men abandoned the guns and escaped down the side of the hill. I was in the CP when our commander, Major Ray, said, "We're going to retake those machine gun positions tonight no matter what it costs." To me that sounded pretty tough. He was probably a good commander, but I was a kid. We recaptured our guns that night intact and took up new defensive positions. One night there was quite an experience for me personally. We had gone to get some food supplies from our camp up on the side of the hill, and as I came back into our campground, people were behind trees and laying low behind rocks. We got back to the kitchen area and said, "What in the world is going on, and what has happened?" A Filipino Army outfit had, without any advanced notice whatsoever, abandoned its positions. The Japanese had moved into those same positions and nobody knew where there was a front line at all. We took up positions on the banks of the Agaloma River, there being no established line in front of us at all. I said to the lieutenant, "Lieutenant, why don't we go across this river?" He said, "Why?" I said, "Well, when they come on top of us down here, it will be a bad time to cross the river." He said, "Young man, we're going to live or die on this spot. We're not crossing the river." That kind of shook me up. As it turned out, later in the night I noticed the river was full of people behind me and I told the lieutenant, "There's people in the river behind us." He said, "That's alright, that's help." People were moving up to take up new defensive lines. So, we really were on the front. We were right in there. We were part of, and sometimes were, the front. Another thing that was terribly frustrating were the snipers. We were in dense jungle. There were trees everywhere and snipers would get up in these trees. They'd tie themselves in the top of the trees and fire at anyone who would walk by. It was impossible for a person to know where they were. Even if you thought you knew what tree they were in and you did hit them, they were tied in and wouldn't fall out, so you wouldn't know if you got them or not. We finally worked out a pretty effective solution to the problem. When we discovered a sniper, we had several Thompson sub-machine guns and we would use them for this problem. Once we spotted a tree we considered suspicious, we'd totally rake the tree with gunfire and that generally solved the problem.

We received some British gun carriers. I believe there were either two or three of them. Since they appeared to be heavily armored vehicles with mounted machine guns, it seemed a logical piece of equipment to use on the entrenched Japanese. Some of the people in our outfit took the bren gun carrier to see what good they could do on the front. Unfortunately, armor piercing shells went right through the thing. We took some pretty bad hits and the bren gun carrier looked like Swiss cheese by the time they took it back. They were very fortunate they escaped with the bren gun carrier in some form of working order.

There were many incidents at the Battle of Agaloma Bay. I am trying to hit the highlights as lightly as I possibly can.

There was a book written shortly after the war. I believe it was *They Were Expendable*. In the book, they mentioned the Battle of the Beaches and talked about our 1st sergeant, sitting there in his rocking chair. In fact, our 1st sergeant did have a rocking chair he was quite fond of. I remember we had some people come down from headquarters from about six miles in the rear. They came to where we were, Everybody was walking around, talking, doing their thing, machine guns were rattling away, the artillery was rattling away—all the noise of the normal battle field. These two guys said they just couldn't believe it. We said, "What do you mean?" They said, "Back in headquarters, everybody is whispering. They sneak behind trees. They run from tent to tent. Down here where the battle's going on, everybody walks around like there wasn't anything going on." It's kind of amazing how things like that happen. I thought that was really unique. We all got a kick out of that and they did too.

The end of the Agaloma engagement was that the Japanese were finally wiped out to the last man. There were two or three prisoners taken, so badly wounded they couldn't have escaped anyway. Other than that, they fought until the very end. They resisted everything and the place was completely perforated with artillery and machine gun fire until the battle was over. Harold K. Johnson, who later became chief of staff of the Army, was a major engaged in this battle. The engagement was successfully terminated and ended with the total annihilation of all the Japanese, a proud moment for soon-to-be prisoners of war.

We remained in Agaloma Bay until we were captured. We experienced no further actual combat. This concluded my personal involvement in combat. Some of the things that went on I think were very interesting, as we lived beside the Agaloma River. Once I saw an enormous python that had captured a large monkey. When I rushed into the woods and fired at it, the python released the dead monkey and slithered off through the bush. My oh my, a boy from Kansas seeing a tremendous python. One night, I was going down a trail to the bathroom wearing my 45 pistol. As I got to the bathroom, there must have been 30 monkeys standing there. Whatever kind they were, they were of a tremendous size, about the size of a six year old child. They were enormous monkeys and as I walked up to the bathroom, they snarled at me. I fired into them and they instantly jumped high in the trees, the whole group of them. It was really an exciting experience for me.

We had great places built where we had our fires and cooked for everyone. The clear Agaloma River ran right by our camp. We had some nice quiet times right after the battle, waiting to see what was going to happen next. Of course, they weren't really nice times. We were apprehensive because things didn't look good; everything was going down hill. Such things occurred as MacArthur leaving the islands, an indication that the situation was hopeless. I remember one particular instance when we had gone after some rations and stopped up the hill above where there was a camp. They were running a radio and I remember hearing President Roosevelt talking about the Philippines and he said, "The men on the Philippines have done better than we expected." From under the trees, I could see our coast lined with waiting Japanese warships, and from the front, I could hear the roar of cannons. I knew what Mr. Roosevelt meant; it should have already happened to us. The end was near. As the circle began to slowly close in on us, people became more apprehensive. We didn't know what was going to happen. We had heard stories of the atrocities that happened to people captured in Singapore and Hong Kong. So the idea we might actually fall was a very terrifying thought. In the beginning, we didn't think there was going to be an important war until we realized we were retreating, until we could see there was probably no other alternative than that we were going to be overrun. We spent our last free days there at Agaloma Bay. It was spring of the year but in the Philippines, spring or summer is year round. There's no cold weather. But this was the dry season. One beautiful day followed another and we could look out at the ocean rolling in from the China Sea. Everything was lovely, and yet the circle was closing slowly on us. The rations got less and less every day. They had been low enough anyway after we had used what we could salvage out of Manila. We got down to where we'd get a little bit of horse meat or maybe a few cans of salmon, a few loaves of bread, and a little coffee. It was obvious they were not going to last long. The ammunition was low. Everyone realized what a strange situation this was, in a beautiful, quiet jungle area where the battle seemed to pass us by or to be mainly in some other area. Ominous things continued—the war ships sat in plain view, we could hear the distant rumble of the cannons at the front, and still we seemed to be sitting in a quiet place. I had read about many times in history like this and now in my own situation, there's no solution to the problem. The situation seems to be it's going to collapse, but at the moment you seem to exist as if it might be like this forever.

I remember just before the end, Chaplain Brown came in. It was a few days before Easter Sunday and the chaplain was going around from place to place. He invited anyone who wanted to attend a service in a little group of trees. The ones who wanted to go sat down, and we had a little Easter service. I don't suppose an Easter service could have more impact than it did at a time like this. It became more apparent every day that we were likely to be sacrificed to the future, to the war, to the situation. We had little hope that we were going to break out of the position we were in. We were going to be captured or die, and from stories we had heard, being captured didn't seem to be a solution to the problem, it seemed only a prelude to death.

There were wild hogs, chickens and so forth that ran in this jungle area. I walked one day along the Agaloma River in beautiful green grassy areas, with great bamboo and mango trees growing. It was an unforgettable sight. One night when we were in a chow line, a wild hog ran through the kitchen area and somebody shot it. They skinned it right down and had some good hot liver. It was strange, the way we lived there. The final night, some fellows and I captured one of those iguana lizards. It was a large monster-type lizard that appeared to be from the prehistoric past. It was an enormous creature that ran out along the edge of the limbs, flew through the air like a bird, and then dropped like a log. It caused a tremendous crash in the jungle and if you weren't used to them, it would scare you half to death. However, we were able to catch or trap them, one way or another. They made pretty good eating. Underneath the stomach area where you cut them open was a large area of fat, which was wonderful for frying. We made pancakes that night and were frying them on a little fire we built. We were near this tree. I really don't know how it happened, but the fire dropped down into the roots of the tree and the next thing we knew there was fire running all the way up the tree to the top. It was the most unbelievable thing I've ever heard seen or could imagine. Here we were, with all these war ships sitting right in plain view, and we had a huge fire burning in the tree. Of course, it was dense, lush jungle, so it only burned in the one tree and no complicated problems occurred.

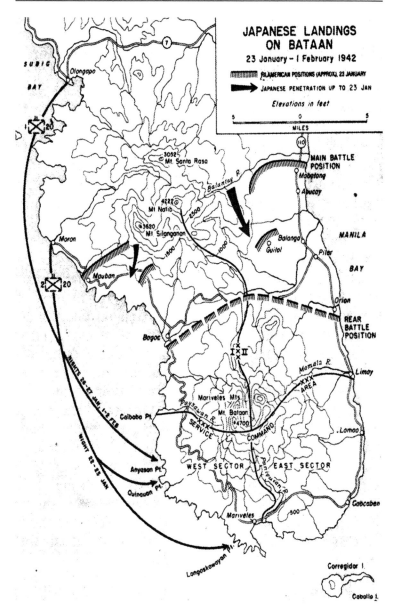

Battle positions and Japanese beach landings on west coast in battle of the points, night of 22 - 23 January 1942 and night 26 - 27 January 1942

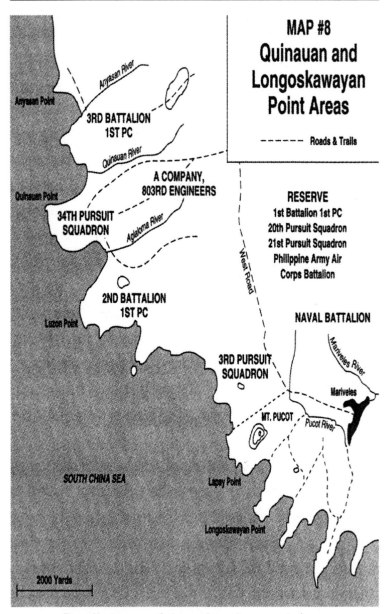

MAP #8
Quinauan and
Longoskawayan
Point Areas

------- Roads & Trails

Anyasan River

Anyasan Point

3RD BATTALION
1ST PC

Quinauan River

A COMPANY,
803RD ENGINEERS

RESERVE
1st Battalion 1st PC
20th Pursuit Squadron
21st Pursuit Squadron
Philippine Army Air
Corps Battalion

Quinauan Point

34TH PURSUIT
SQUADRON

Agaloma River

West Road

NAVAL BATTALION

2ND BATTALION
1ST PC

Luzon Point

Mariveles River

Mariveles

3RD PURSUIT
SQUADRON

MT. PUCOT

Pucot River

SOUTH CHINA SEA

Lapay Point

Longoskawayan Point

2000 Yards

Detailed map of the points, bays and rivers

Chapter Eight

Bataan Falls

We went to bed that night and at about 5 a.m., we heard a call running through camp, "Everybody up." The word was that General King had gone through the lines with full intentions to surrender. We didn't know it that night, but General King had gathered together with his staff and asked the staff, "Is there any effective reason in continuing to resist for another 24 hours? Could we hold out another 24 hours and inflict any serious damage on the enemy at this point? We appear to be out of food and ammunition. They have amassed a well trained and effective army, and are overrunning the remnants of our people, who are almost out of ammunition." We could hear the artillery on the road, and also the retreating tanks that were again carrying out the same type of action that happened at Orani. They would race back a way, set up new positions, fire until the returning fire became too intense, and then withdraw again. We could hear all this roar from the battle fields. It was over and the announcement was that they had gone forward to surrender. Our instructions were to take all of our equipment and destroy it. Everyone was shocked. The tension was enormous. You can imagine the feelings in a situation like this. We began to destroy our weapons. At 7 or 8 o'clock, word came back that General King had returned. He had seen the Japanese and they had told him that there would be no surrender. We were to hold up destroying our weapons. This was traumatic, of course, because most of our weapons had already been destroyed. Another order came down that we should go ahead and destroy the weapons. In fact, even though the Japanese had refused to accept our surrender, they actually had said no conditions, totally unconditional surrender, and each person would surrender on his own, as an individual, to Japanese soldiers as they arrived. It was very scary to think we were going to have to face surrender as an individual soldier, and not be allowed to surrender as a group. They're going to come in among us and we'd have no idea what might occur at that time. We had orders to stay in the kitchen area on the banks of the Agaloma River. We had a Command Post or CP higher on the hill where our orderly room was and where our commander stayed. This is where the central phones were and the records, supply room and such things. We had orders to surrender exactly where we were. Sgt. Godby was in charge. After a few moments I got to thinking. We had all the relics of the battle at Agaloma Bay. Most of the guys had paraphernalia from the Japanese, the trees were lined with Japanese mess kits, the kitchen stove was made out of armor plating from Japanese barges, hats and Japanese belts lay around, as well as Japanese cartridge cases. We were close to the battle field where these people had been buried. I suggested to Sgt. Godby that this would be an extremely dangerous position to be in for surrender. I could imagine these fellows walking right through the battle field and see where their buddies have been buried, and see their belts hanging in the trees and cartridge containers laying on the ground. We'd all be killed, for sure. I convinced him and we moved on up to the CP. There was wild talk and everyone was confused. No one had ever surrendered before. This was a new idea, a fantastic experience, something almost unfathomable for the average soldier to think about, let alone actually do. It was decided that the best thing to do was to go up to the main road. We were deep in the jungle and we might get separated if we stayed in the camp area. Also, the more we stayed together, the safer the surrender might be. We all moved up to the road leading to the main circular road. We were back to the perimeter road that went around the edge of Bataan Peninsula. Kilometer 191 was where we were. We spent the rest of the morning there. Whether it was a last minute discovery or whatever, from somewhere miraculously appeared a great many cases of C-rations. It was probably somebody's private stash. They were holding out, but now realized everything was gone and they became available. In any case, we were able to have a last meal such as C-rations are: canned beans, dried biscuits and things such as that. We waited there and as the afternoon began to carry on, shadows began to lengthen. All of a sudden, we heard a clang and a bang and a lot of racket and we saw some tanks coming. The first thought of course was that the 192nd and 194th tanks were still moving around. Then we realized they were flying the rising sun flag of the Japanese. It was a frightening and scary moment. These were a group of tankers running around and riding on top of their tanks. It was unbelievable, but suddenly they started waving and smiling at us like it was some kind of big party. It was just incredible. We could hardly believe this was the way it was going to happen. A few minutes later, a large truck came along loaded with Japanese troops. The truck stopped and the soldiers got off. Now we were to see the real combat soldiers firsthand, that we had only seen dead or in battle before. Now we saw the real thing, the walking, living Japanese soldier. These fellows were flush with victory. They were happy. It was a beautiful afternoon. The battle was over. They had won and the joy of victory sometimes brings a different personality than you might find under other circumstances. These fellows milled around and in what little English they knew, asked us what we were doing, why we were here, whether we had families or not, inconsequential things you would never think about. It was almost like a news interview. It was difficult to comprehend. I certainly never expected this to be the scene of our capture.

However, this was the end of the benevolent part of our new prison life. It was just a sudden happening on a sunny afternoon in the jungle, the glow of victory for the enemy. It was an interesting experience. It's difficult to explain or understand. It wasn't long before they advised us, through our people, that they wanted us to start walking towards Marvalies. I don't know the exact distance to Marvalies from Kilometer 191. Thinking of it today, it's probably ten miles. We wound down through the jungle, in and around hills with tall trees on either side of the road. It's very hilly country, just inland from the sea. There were wild banana trees, mango trees, trees of all kinds and beautiful green lush jungle. As we passed over the hills and down through the roads, we came over the final hill that led down into the Bay of Marvalies. We could see from our vantage position on a downward slope, Corregidor. Soldiers lined the roads on all sides. Trucks of all types, Japanese trucks, captured American trucks, every imaginable piece of equipment was parked in the ditches by the sides of the road. On the sides of the hills on both sides were soldiers. They were in various positions of repose, either preparing to cook their evening meal, resting, setting up some kind of camp, or one thing or another that soldiers do when not actually engaged in a battle. It was an amazing thing to see. My memories are like some of the actual battles I referred to earlier, incredible to think about. They had great long rifles. I understand that they were called 240s. They had tremendous long barrels. They were great cannons with barrels that appeared to be at least 50 feet long. They may not have been, but to my young mind they seemed to be tremendously long-barreled cannons. They would be set up in batteries, generally of fours. These great cannons were firing away at Corregidor some six to 10 miles away. There were huge salvos of these cannons firing away. Just the roar of all these pieces was deafening. Corregidor began to fire back, which added to the thunderous racket in the area. The soldiers appeared to be almost unconscious of what was going on around them, and were cooking their meals or standing at the side of the road. We began to be harassed by the soldiers. We had no guards, no one leading us, no one protecting us, no one even to talk to the Japanese as we passed by. We did not speak Japanese so we were totally at their mercy. Every few minutes, we would be stopped by another group of Japanese that wanted to search our pockets, harass us in one way or another, pick on us, and take anything they possibly could. By now, everybody had been gleaned of anything of real value. If a person had glasses, they might take the glasses and smash them. They would cuff people around and mistreat them and in general give us some pretty terrific harassment. I did have a pair of glasses which I'd lost, but they were relatively unimportant to me. I'd lost them somewhere in the battle and all I needed was a little help in reading, and I wasn't going to be reading that much. I felt sorry for those fellows who needed their glasses, and now would have to do without them for three and a half years. We wound down the road towards Marvalies. We were finally herded into an area where they had guards. We spent several days there. They furnished us no food. People didn't have much. Some people may have had a few cans of salmon, some may have had a little bag of rice, or something they had managed to carry with them. We were here for either two or three days. The groups did not necessarily stay the same period of time. We were herded into this area in a large group and when they decided they wanted us somewhere else, they would lead us out.

When we finally left this area, we went down into Marvalies itself. I think of that as more like the actual surrender, more like I had expected a surrender to be, more of the feeling we're really there. In Marvalies, there were tanks running around with those colorful flags on them. You saw the enemy in the heat of victory. They lined us up in groups, counted us off, broke us into such groups as they wanted to travel together, and started us down the road. At this time, we were beginning what is known in history as "The Death March." The Death March wasn't one place or one group. It wasn't one specific time or period of time. It was a trip. It was a trip from where we were captured until we arrived at a camp. We were brought out of the hills from various areas, from the Marvalies and the Cab Cabin areas, and were shuttled along. For a few days we weren't always under direct guard. However, a few guards here and there kept us moving. It was a loose deal for several days. The rivers were polluted. There were dead people and animals by the side of the road. Equipment was strewn everywhere. We were passing through the last areas of the battle itself. As we came to Cab Cabin, we were set down in a big park area and sort of relaxed for a few minutes. It was about noon. It wasn't too bad at this time. We thought, oh well, we're going to a prison camp. Maybe they'll take care of us. Maybe things won't be all that bad. We were relaxing in the middle of the day when suddenly several enormous batteries of these 240s began firing at Corregidor. We were sitting in a "V". There was one in the center and one on each side of us. One was centered in front of us and moments after these tremendous guns started firing, Corregidor started returning the fire. Great explosions came as these big 14 inch shells began landing in and around these heavy pieces that were firing. At that moment, I thought they had set us up. They had put us in a position so we would be in the center of this barrage and be killed. They hurried and scurried around and yelled at us to get going. Within a few minutes, they had us in a run going up the road. In thirty minutes, we had escaped from the area and most of the sounds and were now moving down the road.

Battle positions 7 - 9 April 1942

5-HAMI

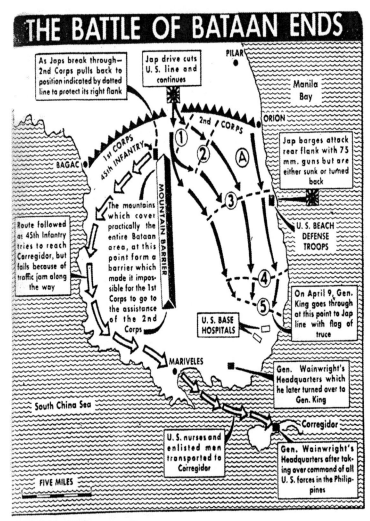

THE BATTLE OF BATAAN ENDS

As Japs break through— 2nd Corps pulls back to position indicated by dotted line to protect its right flank

Jap drive cuts U. S. line and continues

PILAR

Manila Bay

ORION

2nd / CORPS

1st CORPS 45th INFANTRY

BAGAC

Jap barges attack rear flank with 75 mm. guns but are either sunk or turned back

Route followed as 45th Infantry tries to reach Corregidor, but fails because of traffic jam along the way

The mountains which cover practically the entire Bataan area, at this point form a barrier which made it impossible for the 1st Corps to go to the assistance of the 2nd Corps

MOUNTAIN BARRIER

U. S. BEACH DEFENSE TROOPS

On April 9, Gen. King goes through at this point to Jap line with flag of truce

U. S. BASE HOSPITALS

MARIVELES

Gen. Wainwright's Headquarters which he later turned over to Gen. King

South China Sea

Corregidor

U. S. nurses and enlisted men transported to Corregidor

Gen. Wainwright's Headquarters after taking over command of all U. S. forces in the Philippines

FIVE MILES

SURRENDER—On the night of April 4-5 the Japs broke through the U. S. Reserve Battle Position—pushed the left flank of the 2nd Corps' line back to the point indicated by dotted line (1). The 2nd Corps with the 45th Infantry counterattacked in a futile effort to close the line. Another counterattack was launched by the 31st Infantry but this also failed. The U. S. 2nd Corps then withdrew to line (2), and to prevent the pocketing of its men in area (A) was compelled to retreat to line (3). The Japs used the full advantage of their numerical superiority and fresh troops to bear down closely upon the battle weary Yanks, forcing them to fall back successively to lines (4) and (5). At this point every available man was thrown in, but the Japs continued to move forward. The end thus was inevitable.

(6)

The battle ends 9 April 1942

Chapter Nine

THE DEATH MARCH AND O'DONNELL PRISON CAMP

Within a day or two, we arrived in Balanga. Balanga was on the banks of a river where there was a place to wash and clean up a little. There was no food and a lot of people were sick. As far as we were concerned, this was probably the real shove-off point for the Death March itself as it existed, as it really was. After a day or two at Balanga, we still had not been provided with any food. Anything we had to eat was strictly what we could lay our hands on, nothing else. We were stripped of all of our clothes and were totally naked. They took away everything we had. We were told to pile anything we had in rows and the Japanese would come by and pick it up. When we got dressed again, some of the fellows I was traveling with were able to get a bunch of the stuff out of the piles before the Japanese got to them. As we left Balanga, there was a cart by the side of the road and they gave us one rice ball. This is the fifth or sixth day after our capture, and the first time the Japanese have handed us anything to eat. Most people had gone hungry for at least five days. Now we had one rice ball. As we started down the road out of Balanga, we were on the Death March. We were in a group of, I guess, 500. They had us marching in fours.

We began walking up the road that afternoon after leaving Balanga, and it soon became apparent we were in for a struggle, what has become historically famous for its 15,000 deaths. As we went along, it wasn't long until we were being harassed by soldiers who were traveling by in trucks. They would pass close and try to hit us with their rifle butts. The road got longer and hotter, and we were unable to get drinking water. They didn't let us stop for water. We had gone approximately six days without food and now water was becoming a difficult problem. If we tried to get a drink from the artesian wells by the side of the road and if there was anything to dip water with, they'd let you run over and try to fill something with water. In just a few moments, they would charge at you with their bayonets and you'd have to get back in line. We didn't have a very effective method of getting water, particularly with a large group, so most people went without. People were terribly tired, hungry, and run down. With vitamin deficiencies and hunger, they just plain couldn't keep up. People became weary and fell back or fell down by the side of the road. The guards were following along and began shooting or bayoneting people who couldn't keep up. If anyone fell out, he was bayoneted or shot where he fell. It was a tremendous effort to try to keep on, to summon a little bit of energy, but some were too tired to go on. We stopped in the middle of the morning at a little old place where there was some shade and they let us rest a few minutes. I could see the struggle on down the road. Some people began to stagger and stumble, and maybe two who were already too tired to go on would try to help some poor fellow. One man would grab his arm on one side and the other man grab his arm and try to drag him. It seemed that invariably the person being helped would become more tired and weak and would say, "Let me down. Quit bothering me." In the meantime, the two that had taken the person up to try to drag him were being drug down themselves. They'd say, "I can't. Let him down. Let him die." Their own lives were at risk. It became a terrible situation for people who tried to help someone. People became reluctant to even try to go on; they were just too tired. They didn't even want to be drug anymore. I felt the same terrible tiredness and weakness. I wanted to quit, wanted to stop, but I had this drive to survive. When I heard someone being shot or bayoneted behind me, I felt new energy I never thought I had. I don't know how we all made it. I just know we struggled along from place to place, and as I write now and think about it, I recall various events along the side of the road about trying to get a drink. We had a pitcher we would try to get under the spigots. We would run up to a spigot and take turns trying to get our little pitcher of water and then we'd share the water. In the evening, we got into a little old place near Orani where they herded us in. The place had been burned out and there was a lot of ashes. We were tired. It was late at night. We bedded down and the next morning they woke us up and in just a few short minutes, they told us to get up and we started to move out. People started to get out on the road and guards came through, shooting and bayoneting people who hadn't gotten up. It's hard to imagine now even looking back on this terrible struggle, the total disregard for human life, the total disregard for our physical well being, the almost total despair at the time. We struggled on for more miles. Thinking back now, I can remember some of the miles. I can see people standing by the side of the road, trying to give us a little encouragement, once in a while trying to hand somebody a little bit of food or something. Those things come to my mind as I think of our struggle along the road. I believe the next night we finally struggled into Lubao. In Lubao, there was a great tin warehouse where I suppose they may have kept sugar cane or something of that type. We settled in there for the night, and one way or another got our hands on a few scraps of something to eat, which we shared. Three of us were working together: Quintan Kulman, Sgt. Bale and myself. We shared the little things we had. I remember at Lubao there was a tremendously long water line and I was told years later that somebody tried to buck the water line and the guard just went up and bayoneted him to death. The word was the person's name was Hamilton, so later on a lot of people said they were surprised to see me because they thought I had been killed at Lubao. I remember Lubao as an interlude in our struggle. It was shade. It was a little rest. It was a stop. It was an overnight interlude. The next morning we struggled on down this long road, tired and worn out. It was the 11th or 12th day, or however many days it was, but I know it had been at least 10 days and probably closer to 12 we had been struggling since we were captured. I remember topping a hill and looking down a long road ahead; it was fairly straight. I remember struggling along with all these things turning over in my mind, the dead laying at the side of the road, no water, the endless push, the endless killing of the people who couldn't keep up, and the struggle as if we were staggering through a nightmare. It reminds me, in a way, of the stories of Dante's Inferno. I felt as though I was slowly crawling through hell. My life depended on whether I could keep on my feet and keep moving. That afternoon, we shuffled into San Fernando. I remember a little town, the sights and sounds of a village. As we wound through the town, the street turned and there were grass shacks and Filipinos watching from the side of the road. We were the survivors. We were the ones who had arrived at the end of this death march. The death march is recorded with various death rates. The most often quoted is that 15,000 people died in those few days, going from our surrender place to Camp O'Donnell. In San Fernando, we were herded into an enclosure that was a good deal like our rodeo grounds in the United States. There was a fence around it, as if they kept cattle. There was a little shed or two around and a minor grandstand. We were herded as I suppose animals were herded normally, but in this case it was us. We were herded into this area and that evening, we were served an actual mess kit of rice. This was probably the 12th day and we've been given our first plate of food. We were fed that night and bedded down, no, not bedded down, but left to our own devices in this small area, the entire group. Because of our peculiar circumstances, we had to lay down in the middle of this field, this cattle pen. One can imagine the degradation, the inconvenience, the pitifulness of the situation. All these people laying down in the middle of what you would consider in the United States a rodeo corral. There weren't any paths to move about, and no lights to see where you could move. If anyone had to get up in the night, it was virtually impossible to move. We were stymied in position, in the dark, bound on all sides by other human beings occupying the same ground. It appeared that we were at the end of our march and the next morning we were given another mess kit of rice, which was a welcome relief after what we'd been through.

During that day, we were loaded onto railroad freight cars and moved towards our next destination, Camp O'Donnell. The freight cars were hot, crammed and unhealthy, and there were various stories about the fatalities. I'm not personally aware of any fatalities in my freight car. I am only aware it was terribly cramped, hot, and we were jammed into railroad cars with the doors closed. On several occasions the train stopped, the doors were opened, and Filipinos who had gathered by the trains as they came along apparently heard we were on the trains and tried to give us little bits of food and fruits. There was a tremendous outpouring of generosity by the Filipino people. I was deeply impressed, felt very close to the Filipino people at that moment. They were facing the same captors we were. The Japanese were cruel to them, too, and for them, in the face of all this, to try to befriend us was absolutely beautiful in my mind. We finally arrived at Capas and got off the train. We were unloaded, walked to this tiny village, and then were led down the road to O'Donnell. There was a feeling that at last maybe we were finally getting somewhere, maybe we were coming to a prison camp where things would be a little better, but our hopes were to be shattered. This was not a better place. It was the end of the march and we would be able to rest, to stay still for a little while, but it was certainly no refuge for us. When we arrived at Camp O'Donnell, we were led into an area. It was late afternoon and a Japanese officer, whom I was led to believe was the Japanese camp commander, came out and spoke to us. We stood there, many barely able to stand at all, wobbling on their feet, sick from starvation, malaria and other disease, fatigued beyond belief. The camp commander stood up in front of us in his beautiful Japanese uniform, standing there on the platform with his sword, looking out over us in our degradation, our demoralization, our almost total collapse. As we stood weaving around, barely able to stand, he spoke to us. He said, "We are enemies. We shall always be enemies. We've been enemies from generation to generation and we will be enemies forever. You people think you are lucky to have escaped with your lives. I tell you the lucky ones are already dead. I'm interested in only one thing, how many people die every day."

The events that followed led us to believe this in fact was exactly what he meant; he was sincere and meant exactly what he said. Camp O'Donnell was the end of the earth for us. It was the end of the death march. It was a terrible place. As we entered the camp, there were thousands and thousands of Americans and Filipinos pouring in. We had 10,000 Americans on Bataan who surrendered. We had an undetermined number of Filipinos, probably 50 or 60 thousand in the Philippine Army, the Philippine scouts, etc. All these people were pouring into O'Donnell. We passed into O'Donnell and went to the barracks from an old Philippine Army camp that had swalli-type grass roofs and swalli siding. To us Americans, it looked like some kind of temporary summer camp. As we arrived in the area that was designated for us and began to try to get settled in, we found there was some effort being made to feed the people. They assigned us to eating areas and we received some food. We did receive meals at O'Donnell, however, I have just stated the only good thing about O'Donnell, the only thing that was effective and efficient about the camp. Most of the water had to be carried from the rivers. The Filipinos had set it up to carry water in 60-gallon barrels. They had long poles tied to the sides of the barrels and a group of men would put the poles on their shoulders and carry these barrels of water. There was very little water coming through the water system. There were a few spigots, but we would wait hours trying to get a little drink of water. The camp was a place of pestilence. It was a death hole. It was a dying place. It was terrible. People were sick. They were laying under the barracks and were dying. Today, there was a sign outside the camp that says something to the effect that 26 to 27 thousand people died here in approximately six weeks. There were as many as a thousand people dying in a single day. We could see in the morning the long lines carrying the dead to where they were to be buried. I could see them carrying them as far as I could see. They would wrap the dead person in a blanket, tie one end of the blanket to a pole, the other end of the blanket to the other end of a pole, and this way the people were being carried to be buried. The burying situation was terrible because it was a dry season and the ground was very hard. Everyone was ill. No one was in any shape to break the hard ground. They didn't have effective digging equipment, so even attempting to bury the people was a tremendous problem. In the American area, we had people who were dead and stacked in piles waiting to be buried. They'd be stacked sometimes as much as four days before we could get enough people together to bury the dead. I was assigned to a burial detail and one particular time, I passed out. I remember everything got yellow, like real bright sunlight or something, and then

AMI

I'd pass out. I'd be awake and they'd be helping me along again and then I'd pass out again. After I passed out the fourth time they just drug me back to my barracks. This is the kind of situation we were living in at O'Donnell. Anywhere up to 1,000 people a day were dying, nobody to bury the people, and people under the barracks would be dead. In the mornings, they'd go out and drag out the ones who had died in the night. We were drinking polluted water, had malaria, dysentery, diarrhea and no medicine. Everyone had been low on vitamins before we surrendered. We had been on very meager diets and now the diet was worse. On the other hand, we did have some semblance of a camp. People did get together and talk and it was a little better than the death march, even though we were in the midst of endless dying and unburied dead and no hope. When we could see the amount of people dying in such a short period, the idea there would be anybody left alive after any length of time began to seem impossible to believe. I remember Gen. King was in our camp and he got a bunch of us together one day. He talked to us and said, "I want to tell you people that you didn't surrender. Not a single one of you surrendered. I surrendered you. I was on orders not to surrender but I felt there was no way that I could prevent a total and complete massacre without ordering you to surrender. So, I want you to remember for the rest of your lives that you did not surrender to the enemy, I ordered you to surrender. If there is any blame, if there is any falling back, if there's any scapegoats, I will be it." I had tremendous respect for Gen. King after hearing him say that. I was glad we had surrendered, because I could see there was no point in us all being slaughtered on the final day for nothing. We had fought as long as we possibly could, and any further attempt at resistance meant we would have been hacked to pieces for absolutely no reason whatsoever. And although at this moment survival seemed very bleak, I learned in those days that if you expect to live a week, or if you expect to live a month, or if you expect to live six weeks, there's always hope. Everybody always thinks maybe something will happen, maybe all this will end, maybe it will get better.

One day, they took the senior officers away, all colonels and generals. They came in with a group of trucks and moved them all to Tarlac. They asked for people to go along to help them carry their things and help them move. These men were also weakened. They were older men. We were younger men. I was glad to help, glad to be a part of it, and glad to get a ride outside of camp for a change. On the way back we were very fortunate. We stopped in a little village and a bunch of Filipinos came out and sold a few things to people who had money. I was able to buy a large candy bar. Then a little girl came up with two eggs she wanted to sell me. I told her I was sorry but I didn't have any more money, and she said, "Gift" and she gave them to me. I felt a tremendous feeling for the Filipinos. It would be a great feeling of joy for me to know who that little girl was. I wish I had the opportunity today to meet her and be able to talk to her. She must be a grown woman now. She was so kind, so generous. As hard up as they were, she handed me those two eggs. What a glorious feeling for me to meet a person like that. I have a beautiful feeling for the Filipino people to this day.

O'Donnell was a nightmare of death. Something like 27,000 people died in five weeks. It had all the feelings of hell. The man in charge of my barracks for a very short period was Captain Dyees, who later wrote his own book, *The Dyess Story*. He was one of the few people who escaped from the camp. He returned to the United States. He and several others escaped from Mindanao and brought the first information about what was going on, what actually happened after Bataan. The Americans back in the states didn't know. All they knew was the news broadcast that final morning had said Bataan had gone under. When Captain Dyess returned to the states, he was able to tell the story of what really happened to the men on Bataan and Corregidor. For a short period at O'Donnell, he was my barracks commander. In fact, he was quite helpful to me on one occasion. He saved me from a lot of trouble. I feel honored to have known Captain Dyess. Dyess Air Force Base in west Texas is named after Captain Dyess. I could go on and on about O'Donnell and the water, bad food, death everywhere, the bleakness of it, the terror of it, the futility of it, but it did end. And as if anything was possible, it got worse.

Map of the Death March

5-HAMI

Chapter Ten

TWO LONG YEARS IN CABANATUAN

One day they came and said, "Everybody move out." The people who could walk were marched to Cabanatuan. I was considered one of the people not capable of marching. They came in trucks and carried us out. It was a terribly hot day. I rode in a truck all day and finally arrived at Cabanatuan. At Camp Cabanatuan, we were placed out in the middle of a field where we sat down with our things, the heat beating down on us. I was running a high fever. After we got out of the field and were assigned a barracks, I was laying there and decided I was about ready to die. I lay over in the corner hardly moving, realizing the world was going on without me. In my mind, I began to think I wasn't going to live much longer. I heard one of the lieutenants talking, who said, "Is anybody real bad around here?" They had some cookies they were giving out and somebody said, "Well, there's some guys over here that are in real bad shape." They came over to me and tried to give me a cookie but I couldn't eat it. I was completely dehydrated. I couldn't get it in my mouth to chew it. Somebody had some powdered milk. They put a little bit of water in the powdered milk, dipped the cookie in it, and fed the soft cookie to me. Something happened. It cleared my throat, my mouth, and I was able to eat the soaked cookies and drink the rest of the powdered milk. When I got that in my system, I broke out in a sweat all over my body and was a little better. I think at that particular time I was within hours of dying and the only thing that saved me was somebody thinking about me, soaking some cookies, and giving me a little milk. This was the beginning of my life in Camp Cabanatuan, where I was to spend two full years. I will skip over much detail, which I must and should. I want my story to be such that you will have a feeling for the conditions, have a feeling for what happened, for what life was like and what we went through. It's like something you hear about. You say, oh, another war story. People tell war stories all the time. They tell this, they tell that, but in this case, we felt such human degradations, and impossible, unbearable situations were forced upon us.

Cabanatuan was a prison camp known as Prison Camp #1, Cabanatuan, Neuva Vasia, Philippine Islands. I was there for two years and the greater part of my prison life. It was also a death camp in the same manner as O'Donnell. I entered and was put in a barracks with terribly unhealthy conditions. So began my life at Cabanatuan. I was very sick and in a strange mental condition, to the extent it was all very confusing. During the night, I became upset, left my barracks, wandered around and ran into some very strange situations in the camp. There was a barracks where all the lights were on. There were people in there who apparently had lost their minds, another Dante's Inferno. I felt as if I were in the same situation, totally confused, so I stayed at that barracks because the lights were on. I presume I was like a moth, drawn to the light. It seems like a horrible dream to me today as I look back on it. I had a shelter half and I laid down in the grass and pulled it over me. In the morning, the moisture from the air had completely soaked my shelter half. I got up and went back to my barracks. I was in very bad shape, continually collapsing and passing out. We had long lines for the drinking water. You'd line up with hundreds and hundreds people in the drinking water lines. They'd have four or five canteens each and they'd wait there till 11:00 p.m. when the water would be turned off. Then they would have to go back and line up the next day for water, it was like a nightmare. After a few days of this and being in such bad shape, I was transferred to the hospital area. From the hospital area I was moved to the seriously ill, the dysentery area. There were nine barracks, as I recall. There were regular barracks and then the one that was for diphtheria. These barracks are where they sent people who were dying or were expected to die shortly. I went to barracks number two. Number two was not only the dysentery area or the dying area, but was an area no one was expected to return from. St. Peter's ward, number one and zero, were also dying wards that were a place where people were moved for the single purpose of dying. I was in number two. It was approximately the first of July. I stayed there for a year. As far as I know, no one ever went back to duty from that barracks. I think everyone that went in that barracks the day I did died except myself. I know for sure that ten of us went in the day I did, and within two weeks, I was the only one of the ten still alive. The barracks was dysentery and malaria and the people were in terrible shape. The malaria cases would get worse and worse until they went into what was called cerebral malaria. I'm not sure to this day if that was a separate disease or a local connotation, but people would gradually get worse until they went into a coma and died. We found out later, when the Red Cross brought in a little pure plasma, if they'd give them a bottle of plasma, they would at least revive for a short period. These barracks were bamboo slabs and grass roofs, the same type of barracks as the barracks at O'Donnell. We had little paths that ran up in front of each barracks. We had a dining hall in the same area and a small building we used for a chapel. For a bathroom, we dug trenches out beside the barracks. The people were in terrible shape and no medication of any consequence. Eventually, they got some quinine for the malaria. Then we had an outbreak of what was called amoebic dysentery. I was told by my doctor that I had amoebic dysentery and that I was lucky. There was a good chance I would live three months. Everyone counted their time by weeks and days and months anyway, so the doctor's statement was a very encouraging statement to me . It was more encouraging because it meant I still had a little time left for the situation to change, for things to get better. We had terrible problems with flies because it was a dysentery area. With the outside bathrooms being only trenches in the ground, we had enormous amounts of flies. They were in such incredible quantities that it was virtually impossible to believe. We had a mulberry tree in front of the ward or barracks that I lived in and something happened I've never seen in my life. If I hadn't seen it, I would swear it couldn't happen. The flies would collect on that tree in such quantities at night the limbs would hang down like a weeping willow. In the morning when it started getting light and the flies started leaving the tree, the limbs would come back up again. It was unbelievable.

When we ate our meals, our rice and whatever happened to be available to us, namely sweet potato vines, we might get a little bit of sweet potato. However, many of the sweet potatoes were spoiled and had the most horrible, bitter taste to them. The sweet potatoes were cooked in our soup like everything was, including the rice. We also got a few eggplants that were boiled whole, skin and all. It was such a sick looking green soup that if we hadn't been virtually starving to death, it would have spoiled everyone's appetite. I had a good friend from Kansas City who said, "There's just no way I can eat that stuff. My appetite can't handle something as repulsive as that. I just won't eat it. I'll just starve to death." And he did. Later, another case of a young man came in who was a marine and he sat down beside me. He was in the same cubicle as mine. In our barracks, we had a floor in the center and then on each side was a raised platform, about two feet high, on which bamboo slabs were laid out. This is where we laid and slept and lived. This young man sat down with me and said, "I have just eaten my last meal. I won't eat any more of this stuff. I don't have to put up with this." He sat there for 10 days, and one day he asked me to feel something. He said, "Feel this. What's that in my stomach?" I felt of it and determined it was his backbone. He got pretty upset that day, was spitting up a bunch of green stuff, and, of course, it was too late to do anything for him. He died. People lived and died like that; we were really down to basics, down to starvation. We were down to where people just couldn't live with the situation; they couldn't stand it. We also got poorly cooked rice. People who were assigned to the kitchens knew someone who organized the kitchen system and figured if they found work in the kitchen, they might have an opportunity to survive. It was an unfortunate situation. Among our group were a number of people who were cooks by profession, or at least had been cooks for the Army, and might have prepared us more healthful food . But they weren't assigned to the kitchens. It was not unusual to get burned rice, scorched rice, raw rice, and many times all at the same time. They had a problem to the extent they were using large pots to cook in that were also used by the Japanese and the Filipinos – —a type of bowl we know as woks. Our American cooks were unfamiliar with these types of bowls and didn't have instruction on how they were operated. It was a learning process and a poor time to be learning. The dying continued at a great rate. It was not unusual for my barracks of 125 men to wake up in the morning and find five, six, or seven people dead. In fact, it was the morning routine for the medics to come down to check our barracks and find out how many dead there were and take them out.

I lived in barracks number two in the dysentery area of Cabanatuan during the period of the highest death rate. One of my friends from my outfit was visiting the hospital area where I lived. Mullins stopped by to see me and we visited for quite a while sharing what we knew about other people in the outfit. He told me how good I looked and that I would be alright. He came back about 10 days later and looked surprised. He said, "Hamilton, are you still alive?" He said he checked the burial detail for four days and decided he must have missed me. That gives you a rough idea of what I looked like in my emaciated state of about 80 pounds. I had started the war at about 160 pounds. Now, I knew for sure how rough I looked that day he first visited me.

The so-called morgue was in our area because as they became bad, they were moved to our area. Almost everyone died in our area. The burial detail moved out in the mornings with 50, 60, or 70 people to be buried. They were carried out on stretchers or platforms. They had a handle on each corner and four men would carry them. The man who had died would be placed on the stretcher with all clothing removed. No clothing went to the burial grounds because the living needed it. It was kept and an attempt made to clean it up and redistribute it to people who needed it. The people were carried naked on these platforms to the graveyard. For a long time, the Japanese refused to allow us to have any type of service at the cemetery. The burial detail dug a hole and each day's dead were buried in a single hole, which made identification of the dead later extremely difficult, if not impossible. Also, as the rainy season arrived, we had no good way to dig in the soggy, wet ground. If we did, we just dug up more mud because the ground was saturated. It was almost impossible to get the corpses to stay under the ground. This gives some idea of the dying and the pitiful conditions in which we took care of those who died.

We finally, I believe about December of that year, received some Red Cross packages. Not only did we receive Red Cross packages, but the plasma I mentioned earlier came.

We received various medical and other supplies with the Red Cross packages. We got a box and it seems to me it contained seven packages of cigarettes, about three cans of meat, some cookies, some chocolate, bouillon, some malted milk balls, and various other things. I remember we had canned pork and applesauce. The package was about the size of a large shoe box and was tremendously beneficial to us. As we got these Red Cross boxes and started eating them and using them in our diet, it slowed down the dying. We had lugoa-cooked rice, kind of like soft oatmeal every morning. It was cooked to a soft mush and that's what we had for breakfast every morning. We had a dip of hot, sloppy rice like thin oatmeal. Such things as the bouillon powder, we would shake a little bit of it in and stir it up in the rice and it greatly enhanced the taste. To some extent, the conditions in Cabanatuan began to improve and the death rate began to recede. Just prior to receiving the Red Cross items, we had approximately 200 people die from dyptheria. The ward next to me was the dyptheria ward. We had a big typhoon in October. It rained and blew for three days. We closed down the sides of our barracks and did everything we could to keep from blowing away and tried to keep everyone cheered up enough to survive mentally. After the typhoon was over, I had a terrible sore throat and was feeling especially bad. The doctor looked at me and said I had dyptheria. They moved me over to the dyptheria ward. Two hundred people had just died in there. When I left my barracks, the people there said, "Gee, you'll make it. Don't worry Hamilton. You'll be alright." I know they never expected to see me again. No one ever expected me to come back. They all expected me to die. Fortunately, the Red Cross material came and I guess the dyptheria serum must have been with it. They had not had any serum before but now they did. I was given injections and after a short period I began to improve. More people died of dyptheria while I was there, but I improved and got well.

It was different from my other barracks. It faced directly out onto the parade ground area in the middle of the camp. There were benches set out like an old country porch, which was a tremendous change. The other barracks were just grass buildings. I have no idea what these particular buildings were built for. Maybe they were for officer's quarters. They were more American style in that they had rooms, a porch and wooden floors. I sat on this wooden porch with the sun shining down on me. A bunch of Japanese soldiers took their basic training right in front of this porch. They would do their marches and practice there. They had bayonet practice and then they'd practice their runs. They ran and jumped in the mud, things soldiers do in basic training. I had the rare occasion to have a spectator's seat to watch a Japanese soldier take his basic training. It was an amazing experience for me, and I was certainly glad to have this opportunity. They wouldn't put on raincoats when it rained because they were doing it the hard way. As I sat there, it was determined I had one of the worst cases of pellagra they had ever seen. My knees swelled up in great enormous water blisters. The backs of both of my hands became one single enormous, red, water blister. They swelled out a half an inch from the back of my hand. Pellagra is a disease of the nervous system and skin. It will totally destroy the brain and the nervous system. It's a terrible disease and the doctors said that they had never seen a worse case. They did have some medication they give for this disease. I forget exactly what it was, niacide or something like that. I presume this came with the Red Cross material that we got. Again, I was miraculously saved as I had been saved from dyptheria.

I think this is one of the most miraculous parts of my story. For people who hear my story, whether it be my children, grandchildren, my great-grandchildren, or just casual friends or relatives, I want everyone to know about the incredible, charmed life I lived. I survived inconceivable near death experiences when it seemed impossible to do so.

I had unimaginable things happen to me again and again from the beginning of the war until I was released. I was always lucky. I always got the breaks. Every time I didn't have a chance, I got a break. Every time I should have died, I lived. I should have died many times and I didn't. I lived when it was impossible. It must have been the grace of God that saw me through. A person thinks of these things. How could I have been so lucky? Then on the other hand, maybe God was looking after me.

Also, I had malaria. My malaria was terribly bad and I became paralyzed. I couldn't move my legs. I couldn't get out of bed, get a drink or anything. The one lucky break I had was the people looking after me. I figured that my days were at an end. Paralyzed as I was, I wouldn't be able to move or look after myself. I'd starve to death and die. Gradually, with the influx of the Red Cross and the help of friends, I started to get my strength back and my paralysis went away. Again, I was saved from certain death. Now, thinking about the enormity of the situation, it's just appalling how many times I was in a death situation and survived. I lived in this dysentery area, or dying area of Cabanatuan, for nearly a year. It's amazing to think how so many people died and I had so many near death experiences.

We had a little door sill, probably not over four inches high. We were all so weak that the average man in my barracks could not step up over the door sill walking straight ahead. In our weakened condition, we could barely lift our legs. I find it difficult to believe myself. It seems as if it must not have been so, but it was. What we did was come to the door, carefully turn sideways and lift one foot up. It was easier to lift a foot up sideways than to lift it up straight ahead.

In barracks number two or ward two in Cabanatuan where

I lived in the hospital area, I never knew a single person who left there alive, except for me. We lost from five to seven men a day, from dysentery and malaria mostly. One of the people from the ward was lying out on the ground and suddenly he called out in a loud voice, "Someone help me up! I want to walk around one more time before I die!" Two guys helped him up, walked him a short way, took him back and laid him down. In less than 10 minutes, he was dead. People in such a weakened condition seemed to realize their end was near.

I look back on those times in this death area, and I can't believe what happened, what I saw and what it was like. If I say I have some fond memories of that place, you will surely think I've lost my mind, and maybe I have. Maybe it was the comradery. Maybe it was the togetherness of suffering together. Maybe it was the companionship in our degradation as we sat there. Some people would sit and think; I would, too. It was not so much the sitting, because I wouldn't want to do anything or walk anywhere. When I explain about not being able to lift a leg over a door sill, one can understand why all I could do was sit and think and wonder about it all. I remember those times. We had a little chapel and I would go there in the mornings. I remember the pretty mornings. I remember waking up and hearing the dogs barking in the night. I remember the experiences and looking out across the fields in the morning, looking up at the mountains. As impossible as it seems, I have some pleasant memories of such a place at certain times.

I remember the friends I had. A very good friend of mine, I believe his name was Johnnie Freman, from New York City, was in the dysentery area of the hospital where I was living. As he slowly lost ground and got weaker and weaker, I could see he wasn't going to make it. One day he said he was about to die. He said he had a pair of shoes and he knew as soon as he died someone would grab them. He told me to take them

83

with me and when he died, they would be mine. He was Catholic and the most important thing to his mother would be that he had the last rites. So he told me to please tell his mother he did have the last rites. I took his shoes and hung them over my bed until he died. After the war, when I returned home, I wrote his mother and told her the story. She sent me a blanket for Christmas and thanked me very much. What a nice thing to do.

I lived there for about a year. Then I was moved to the upper area of the hospital. This was an interesting barracks. They called it "Caribou Corral". Some of the guys had gone to a lot of trouble and built an awning out like a little restaurant. They had built small chairs and tables. It was really a strange affair. I was terribly lucky to have been assigned to this barracks where people had done so much work to make it liveable, but interesting. I remember we'd go get our little nothing to eat and sit down at these tables to eat. There was a gentleman there, a civilian, who said he had been on the stock exchange in the Philippines before the war. He said he was a very rich man and was used to the niceties of life. He would come and pull his chair out and sit down at his little table with his mess kit. He didn't have a tie, but he would always button up the collar of his shirt so that he would feel dignified and that he was living like a gentlemen. I stayed in this barracks a while and enjoyed it. I don't know how long, maybe three weeks to a month, but it was very interesting.

I even had my teeth worked on. If people had silver coins, they would pulverize the coins and make fillings out of them. They had a little dental drill they ran with a pedal. It was really unique. I had a tooth filled that way. I don't remember the circumstances but I had it done. Strange things happened in these conditions.

The Japanese decided to invite some Filipino girls out to the camp to entertain them for the weekend. Maybe the idea was to humiliate us. Anyway, they had a bunch of young girls out from the town. The girls started singing a few songs. Suddenly, they were singing "Auld Lang Syne." All the guys in camp felt that these girls, in their way, were trying to tell us we had not been forgotten. The Filipinos were thinking about the Americans and were worried and concerned about us. I tell you, that gave me a wonderful uplift.

I was listed as having amoebic dysentery in the hospital. The doctor told me I should live at least three months. That was in approximately July. In December, I received some medication for my amoebic dysentery. It was Yeatrin and Caboson. I may be wrong, but that is as my memory serves me. Earlier, one of the doctors decided he would run an experiment. He was going to check the results and write a paper on it for after the war. He gave a bunch of us Epicac. He placed the Epicac in heavy plastic covers so they wouldn't disintegrate until they were in the intestinal tract. He had us lay down for as long as the treatment lasted. I don't really know if that was an effective cure, but it's just possible it cured me. After I received the treatments, I never had it again to my knowledge.

I was returned then to the regular side of the camp, the non-hospital side, the duty side. Over on the other side, we lived in a different world. It wasn't that much better, but with Red Cross packages and working on a farm, physically digging it up by hand and getting some of the vegetables, generally speaking, it was better. With the Red Cross medication, the death rate dropped off tremendously and life was a little better, not as bad as it had been. On that side we had guards on guard posts. They were up approximately 40 feet in the air around the outside perimeter of the camp. In Cabanatuan, the guards were not stationed inside the camp, but watched from the outside. When they felt it was important, they would enter the camp and check on us, search us, or whatever. In the day-to-day routine of life, the Japanese were not mixed directly in with us. When we had to go to work on the farm, we would be let out of a gate and be under the direct supervision of Japanese guards, back to all their brutality and harsh treatment. We became more acclimated. The death rate slowed down. We were doing things to make our lives considerably more tolerable. We were able to plant little gardens by our barracks. I don't know if anyone ever gave us permission or not, but we did. We lived in a much-improved situation. They would give us lists and tell us we could order things, however, it was a very ineffective ordering system. Our soldiers were supposedly being paid 10 cents a day if they worked, which meant we got a little bit of money that we were able to use to order things. An egg was something like 50 cents and if we ordered on the long order list, they would fill it very sparsely. It didn't make any difference. We had to put up the money to order and if something didn't come in, you couldn't switch. If we ordered chicken eggs and got duck eggs, we were just out of luck. Anyway, ordering from commissary lists was a total guess by golly, but it was at least some help.

There was, although it was only known by certain people, money being smuggled into the camp. Certain people were recipients of the money, but the mere fact that money existed allowed for certain situations. We could buy and sell things we might have in our possession such as items out of our Red Cross box, for example, cigarettes if we didn't smoke. People with larger amounts of the money tended to accumulate the money for other purposes. On the farm, the Japanese requested so many farmers for the day. Our people would tell them various reasons why we couldn't furnish everybody they wanted. They would come back with a quota for so many people today, say 3,000. If in fact, we really had 3,400 people who could have worked, then 400 people didn't have to go. There were various methods or rosters to show if it was your day off. We did get days off from time to time. On these days off we were able to work for someone else who had money, but who wasn't off. Through these complicated ways, extra money was available. We did have a certain amount of underground activity and were able to buy and sell different things that were of great importance to us. If anyone got a hold of a little money, they'd hold on to it tenaciously until they were able to buy something they wanted.

I lived in two areas on the duty side. When I first went over, I lived in the lower area down by the front gate. One morning we woke up, went out of our barracks and there were some poles out at the front gate. On each one of these poles, a Filipino head was sticking on top of the pole. The Japanese were great in toting the idea of co-prosperity of Asia for the Asiatics. We thought, what a great way to enhance their position with the Filipino people. .

I was later moved to the upper area of the camp near the farm. We had nice barracks at the high end of the area. It was clear and had a nice view. I liked it much better. As I said, money did exist and it seems strange to think about and how much of it was around. In our barracks, there were several gamblers. Our life living in the so-called gambling barracks was exhilarating. We were like a little Las Vegas, an extremely unique thing for a prison camp after all the horrible, degrading things we had. It was a stimulating time. The food was better and we had some farm items. The death rate was way down and we were living better. The two main gamblers set up operations in our barracks which attracted gamblers from all over the camp with money. With two gambling set ups, people would come in for the night's big games. We didn't have lights so they'd play by moonlight. These were tremendously big games. Around my barracks, little groups would pick out areas against the outside walls of the barracks. Four or five people would band together and stake out a certain area. I was lucky. I had four or five friends. Several of them were quite large people who knew everything that went on in camp, such as who was the strongest and toughest. It made my area pretty secure. Canaly and Kirkcheck both ran gambling tables. Canaly had the area in the middle of the barracks. Our barracks was in the southwest corner of the camp. We had a good area staked out. He told us if we'd like to, he'd build us a nice table we could use when he didn't have a game going. When a game was on, we would clear the table and he would use it for his games. It worked out nice because he hired a carpenter and had a beautiful table built for us. Having all these games going was good for this barracks. We had a lot of people around with money. When we had a day off, there was always somebody who could hire us to work for them. This allowed people who lived in our barracks to earn money when a lot of others in the camp didn't have any. A captain out of one of the tank outfits was our barracks chief. One day he got all concerned and said, "Boy, if I go home and they talk about this barracks being a big old gambling den and everybody got beat out of their money, that will just be terrible. I'm going to stop these games. I'm going to order an end to this." Canaly said, "Oh come on Captain, gee, this is good for the barracks. Everybody likes it. It's really good for us. The men like it and it's good for all of us." The Captain said, "I really don't think so." Canaly said, "Well, why don't we have a vote on it." Captain said, "Okay. Let's vote on it tomorrow." So during the night, Canaly bought a big cake, and brought in a big can of coffee which we never had. While he served cake and coffee, he told all the guys in the barracks that he never worked on the farm. Why? Because he hired somebody to work for him every day. He said, "Any time I need a farmer, we'll always use one of the people in the barracks first. You'll have first priority on every job that comes up. Gambling is good for this barracks." Sure enough, we took the vote and kept the gambling. I think it was right for our barracks. We had people with money. We were able to buy more things. To tell you the truth, it was kind of exciting with the big games going on. I didn't participate because I was not a card player, but I enjoyed the extra money.

We had two tremendously experienced prize fighters. One was Chick Johnson. He was a professional fighter before the war and had a lot of big fights. He was well known. The other one was an All Pacific Champion, I'm not sure of his name. It was a tough world and the toughest made out. If we were tough enough to push someone around, we could kind of push anybody around because there wasn't that much authority; it was almost nonexistent. The Japanese didn't want us to sleep outside on the ground. On hot nights, a bunch of us were always sleeping out on the ground. The Captain came along and said, "All you guys are going to have to move inside." Chick said, "Captain, it's too hot to sleep inside, there's no reason why we should. We're going to sleep out here. We're not going to go inside." The Captain said, "Boy, I'll look you up tomorrow." Chick said, "Captain, just hope I don't look you up first." This is kind of the way we lived. If we were tough enough, if we had a good organization, if we hung out with people who could really stand up for themselves, then we didn't get pushed around. I'm not saying there was a lot of disorder, but it was a lot easier if we had local power under our own roof.

We did have a nice little garden by our barracks. When the Japanese came inside the gate, someone would holler "Air raid." We would hide anything that might be considered contraband, anything that might be searched for. These little gardens were always kept nice with the ground raked fresh. When they would holler "Air Raid," if there was anything we didn't want the Japanese to find we would run out, dig a little hole in our garden and re-rake it quickly. When they came by, they never saw anything but a nice raked garden. Little victories like that were pretty nice.

We had a dog that ran around the camp that the 4th Marines had brought out of China, from Su Chow China. They had been stationed in China before the war and he was a nice fat little dog, kind of a mascot, a friend to everyone. Su Chow lived somehow and the Marines did get him home.

We had these empty big 5-gallon oil cans that came with shortening in them. Once they were empty, we'd put handles on and set them out with water in the sun. Although it never got cold, the water would heat in the sun and at night we could take a bath by taking our canteen cup and dipping the water out and pouring nice warm water over us, even if it was chilly in the evening. If some unfortunate cat wandered through camp and didn't know any better, it would end up drowning in one of those cans and be somebody's stew the next day. We got food where we could. Things were very basic. In fact, later on the rice ration was cut. We had a nice little papaya tree in our garden. It takes about 18 months until it has papayas on it. A papaya grows to about the size of a big cantaloupe or a small watermelon. They grow up the plant with the ripe ones on top. Then there's always a smaller one coming along a little further down. They are a nice plant with a ripe papaya on top. When you pick it, you have another one ripening right behind it. They are just like chicken eggs; they just seem to keep coming; they're really a terrific plant. When the rice rations were cut, the first thing we knew the green papayas started going. The guys were stealing them and after they got all the papayas, they would cut the trees down, split them open and eat the tree. It seems kind of funny now, but I can tell you we were pretty mad when we found out somebody had stolen and eaten our tree.

A good friend of mine in my squadron, who had gone ashore with me the day we stopped in Hawaii and had a good time, was killed by the Japanese. He was working on the farm and acting sick. Late in the afternoon, he wandered off and walked away from the work. No one knew just what happened; whether he didn't know what he was doing or what. The Japanese decided he was trying to escape so they gouged out his eyes, broke both his legs and arms, and disemboweled him. Then they brought him back to camp for us to see so we wouldn't try to escape.

I think of so many things about the camp. We had chapel services and plays, and had regular church services. We almost formed a church. There was a membership list and we signed up almost like joining a church. We had song books but they were censored. The "Battle Hymn of the Republic" was cut out because they didn't want us to sing it. Other than that, they pretty much left us alone. We had interesting plays and movies; some people were real comedians. They'd do some really good shows, downright funny.

We were in was the province of Nueva Vicya. The Japanese came to our shows and always grabbed the front row seats, which irritated us, but we were pretty understanding. They felt a little uncomfortable being in there with all of the prisoners, and that was fine, too. They'd come and take the seats right in front of the stage. We had a tendency to call the Japanese "slope heads" when we wanted to say something derogatory. One of our comedians said, "Here I am tonight in Cabanatuan. I have performed before the crowned heads of Europe. Tonight, I perform before the slope heads of Nueva Vicya." Everybody cheered and clapped and the poor Japanese didn't know what was said, so they clapped and cheered too. We had lots of funny things like that happen. We got a kick out of it and a lot of snickers out of a deal like that.

We had people try to escape and they were executed. In fact, two guys who were executed hadn't escaped. They were asleep under the barracks. There was a roll call every night and they turned up missing. They couldn't be found. When the Japanese did finally locate them, they took them out to the edge of camp and made them dig their own grave. The next night when they called roll, we all had to stand out there

91

and watch while they shot them and rolled them into the graves they had dug themselves. We had a lot of things like that happen, a lot of tough things that went on. I guess I got to where I liked living on the duty side and all the beautiful moonlit nights. As we didn't have any lights in the barracks after dark, we always sat outside. We had time to visit and be with friends. I lived with these people 24 hours a day, 7 days a week. They didn't go anywhere and neither did I. I visited with them, ate with them, talked with them, dreamed with them, talked about our pasts, our futures, and told jokes together. We truly lived together. Today people say, "Why do you guys feel you have so much in common?" I lived with these people so close together in a life and death situation, our dreams and hopes were together, and I like to compare it to the Battle of Gettysburg. The people who fought at Gettysburg returned every year, as long as they lived, for an encampment at Gettysburg until there were only five people left. They had such a camaraderie from the Battle of Gettysburg all those years, that both North and South returned to the battlefield for an encampment. When I think that they did that after only a three day battle, I can fully understand the camaraderie, the togetherness and the feeling of brotherhood. We spent three and a half years with our people, endlessly, day and night. They went nowhere, I went nowhere and we lived all our life and death experiences together. We shared our hopes and dreams, our past and future. I'm kind of trying to explain about why we feel such an attraction to each other. Even when we didn't really know one another, we didn't know a particular person in the camp, when we realized we were from the same horrible place, it's like going to the same college, but so much more than that.

We ran a great farm that we worked on at Cabanatuan, about 600 acres. It was an unbelievably complex affair. We had two complete irrigation systems. Farmer Jones ran the farm. He was an American officer and he organized and planned it with the help of the Japanese. I understand that several of the Japanese were agricultural experts. Jones primarily worked the personnel. He saw that everybody took their breaks, went to work, and got off when they were supposed to. His name was Jones so we called him Farmer Jones. The farm was quite an experience. We dug up the ground with pick mattocks. We would dig with the big picks and a Japanese we worked for, his name eludes me at the moment, would say, "No, stand up on no goodoo." He didn't want us to straighten up our backs when we were picking, so we had to swing with a bent back. This made the work tremendously difficult because if we could stand up and make a full swing, it was not all that bad. Another thing about this guy was he loved snakes and ate them. We had these great enormous ant hills that were eight to 10 feet high and we'd have to tear them down. They were about every hundred feet apart and were all over. When we tore them down they would be full of ants, and most of them would have a cobra in it. So whenever we'd find a cobra, we'd have to tell him and he'd holler, "Snakee, snakee, snakee." We'd have to catch the cobras for him. He had a little rope around his neck that he'd tie the cobra up with and when the day was over, he'd go dragging it home with him. We had quite an experience one day. This guy wasn't too darn smart. He was kind of a character and he tied a cobra up near where we were dipping water. One of the boys went down there and as he was bending over to get a bucket of water, the cobra struck at him. Fortunately, the rope was short enough and it didn't quite reach the guy.

Of course, we were still prisoners, we were still beaten from time to time for various things, but the death rate had fallen to a pretty low level and we were all living a fairly relaxed life. Things were fairly nice. We had our little gardens. We had to go to work every day but it was a pretty place. Cabanatuan had no winters. Off to the east was a high mountain range with trees on top. We'd had the beautiful nights with big, clear, full moons, and the moon would come up over the mountain tops. We could see the trees outlined against the moon as it rose over the mountains. We grew quite a few things on our farm. We had okra, eggplant, cosavi, gabi, beans, corn, sweet potatoes, green beans, rice, and what we called a java melon, one of the most delicious melons I've ever tasted. I always said it was a cross between a cucumber and a cantaloupe, but anyway it was delicious. We worked on our farm and worked a few caribou. We plowed the rice paddies and had a small area where the Japanese had an experimental farm with the most beautiful snow white brahma cattle. Of course, we didn't get anything out of that but it was part of the scene so it added to the atmosphere. We also grew talelium, a green used like spinach, but it had quite a different taste and was delicious. We had characters there for our guards. We had Donald Duck and people that we had trouble with in one way or another. One time we were way out on the farm and Farmer Jones would yell things. He had a tremendous voice. If you were in the farthest corner of the farm and he'd tell them to take a break, everybody could hear that, but when he'd say go back to work, it seemed like people had trouble hearing. We were coming in from work one day and he hollered out, "Everybody bring in a rock." I'm sure the Japanese told him to have everybody bring in a rock from work. There were a lot of rocks on the farm so everybody was bringing in their rock. I'd selected a fairly small rock and was headed back. Four or five guards were hiding behind a building and were looking for somebody with a little rock. When they spotted me, I guess they thought I qualified and signaled for me to come over. They had their big sticks and were going to beat up on me. Just about the time I got there, they spotted another guy who hadn't picked up a rock at all. I got out of that one, but we would get beat up for various things every so often, for most anything.

One time I tripped over a stump or something, a plant and part of the plant broke off. I was knocked down and thoroughly beaten for that. So even though things had gotten pretty nice at Cabanatuan, relatively speaking, the guards were just as brutal as ever if they thought the condition called for it. They hadn't reduced their brutality or anything like that, it's just that things had gotten better to the extent we weren't dying of starvation any more. One time a group of us were taken to one of the old barrios out behind the farm to pick up some fertilizer. It was a fun trip. We lined up the detail and marched out to this barrio and picked up our boxes of fertilizer. The boxes looked like the same things we carried the dead in to the cemetery. The boxes were scrap wood and had a handle on each side, so four people could get a shoulder under all parts. It was interesting to go to this little barrio and see how the people lived. Everybody had a grass house of four poles tied together, with more poles across the four poles, then bamboo slabs across those so they had a floor. On these floors, they would take a coconut shell and polish them to where they looked beautifully waxed. Dust or anything else would fall down between the slabs. It was a fabulous way to keep house and have a nice shiny little place. They seemed so cool out there on the, well, we'd say prairie, but it was out in open country. Breezes blew across the open countryside. The bamboo houses had a small artesian well in the center of the barrio where they kept their rice. It looked like an ideal place to be living, with a nice relaxed life.

Time passed. We raised and harvested our crops; we had a nice operation on the farm. Then they decided they wanted to build an airport nearby. I went to the airport area many times. It was different from the farm, a different experience for me. I actually got to stand side by side with Japanese soldiers and saw how they looked in every detail. I could see this little guy standing there. Somewhere I got this ridiculous idea they were invincible, almost like gods, so tenacious and

95

fierce and dedicated they just couldn't lose. They became to us, in many ways, not only demons but bigger than life. It was an experience to stand beside one of these guys, look him over and see exactly what he was. He wore old rough hide shoes that crinkled up at the toes, leggings wrapped up to his knees, and old britches his leggings fastened to. It was an incredible sight. We were used to the U.S. Army where nothing was ever patched. Nobody but nobody had a patched uniform. But in the Japanese Army, it was absolutely standard to see the knees of their uniform patched. They took a patch, put it behind the hole and with a sewing machine ran it back and forth, over the knee until it was sewed up tight. The seats of their britches might be exactly the same way. To see him so close up, to see his belt, he had little leather cartridge container on his belt that was convenient to reach and carried most anything. They wore bayonets and had shirts with insignia on the collar. The cap was a baseball type, the same color as their uniform. There was a little leather strap around the front of the cap and down behind hung a piece of cloth of the same material as the cap. This would hang over his neck as if he had a handkerchief on the back of his hat that created cooling shade. I wanted to give you a picture of this experience of seeing them up close, seeing exactly what they were, hearing them talk to each other, and look at each other. It was good to have had this personal experience. Some people fought them for years and had never seen the real man.

We would go on this detail to the airport area in the morning. We'd line up and march off across the field. It was new area. The trip was welcome after being locked up for so long. Their field engineer wanted us to flatten off a hill. I thought it was unique, the way they were working. They had little pegs and flags in the ground where they wanted us to cut. We cut grades through the center of the hill to where they were marked. It was like small tunnels or gulleys. Then they laid mine car railroad tracks through the area. We'd run these railroad cars up, dig down and fill the cars. When the track was on the exact level they wanted the airport to be, we cut the rest of it down to the railroad tracks. Where it wasn't close to the tracks, we'd wheel barrow the dirt up to the tracks and put the dirt in the cars that would carry it away. Here we were grading an entire airport by hand which I thought was kind of interesting. Of course, anything different was fun.

Another detail I got on was the wood detail. We cooked with wood. The trip was fun. We went way up in the jungle, kind of like a picnic. They took rice along with other things and we cut wood all day. That was a joyful experience. What we cut were mahogany trees. It was interesting to think we were actually cutting mahogany trees down for wood. Another time, they were making a movie. The name of the movie was "The Birth of Freedom." They took a bunch of us way up in the hills. Again, it was like one huge picnic. We had the experience of seeing their top soldiers. They brought a combat outfit up to be sure we didn't escape into the hills. They were deployed around the outside perimeters. We got to see some of their top fighting people all in position. In the center of all this, it was like one big picnic. We brought our lunch. They had movie cameras and went through all sorts of things. They had smoke bombs and other things they would throw into the area when they were filming the war movie. Here we were, part of a war movie. I got a real kick out of it. It was a nice change from the routine of prison life.

We had all kinds of things at Cabanatuan. We had our shows, our church, and there was actually a radio in camp. I didn't realize it at the time, but later on in books I've read, some details came out. I don't know who had the radio; they didn't want anybody to know. It had been made from spare parts. We heard a lot of news but we never knew what was real and what was rumor. People have asked, "Did you get any news when you were in prison?" and I'd say, "Yeah, we got all the news, I believe, and we got lots of rumors, too." I think we got almost all the news along with the rumors and it was our problem to try to figure out which was which.

Eventually, the rice rations and food were cut down, but even though things did get tighter, it was fairly good in Cabanatuan prison camp for a short period. We had bed bugs in our beds. We pulled the slats out and they'd be loaded with bed bugs. There are routine things that happened with this type of close living together, very little to eat and almost nothing to do except visit and talk with one another. Time went on, it wasn't all that bad.

Graves at Cabanatuan

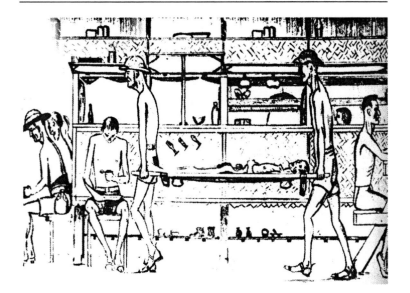

Cabanatuan Hospital Ward 7

Camp life

99

Cabanatuan Prisoner of War Camp

Chapter Eleven

BILIBID PRISON

Then came the summer of '44. There had been some groups of men going out to Japan, and I thought boy, I don't want to go to Japan because one of these days, the Americans are going to come. The Americans will be released, I'll be clear in the heartland of Japan, and no telling how long this war will go on. I'll be stuck there and a lot of prisoners will already be released. But then I began to realize that wasn't the way to look at it. The Japanese are going to try their darndest to get us out of here or kill us whenever the Americans come. The best thing was to try to get into Japan itself and when the war ended, that would be it. Here, there would be some kind of terrible march or something bad at the last minute when the Americans were coming. It turned out this was a pretty good evaluation of the situation. On those last ships they tried to get out and almost everybody was killed. The story of those ships is not mine, but they're terrible stories. The ships were attacked at sea and a high percentage of them died on the way to Japan. So I got the idea, "Gee, I ought to get out of here." So a detail came up and they wanted 500 men to go to Japan. I was still being carried as amoebic dysentery. I had to take a test to see if I was cleared because they wouldn't take anybody to Japan who was listed as amoebic dysentery. I rushed to get myself tested and cleared and I was approved to go. I don't know the exact day we left. A few days before we left, somebody brought a Manila newspaper into camp, and in it was the story of the landings in France, the D-Day landings. Once we were selected, we got our things ready to go. We left on a train which was like the other experiences I told about, the wood detail and the movie. We were going to do something different, to get out and see something different after being locked up for years. Riding in an old freight car to Manila was an exciting time. When we got to Manila, they unloaded us from the trains and it seemed there was always a bunch of Filipinos standing around watching. This was nice because we were glad they were interested enough to look at us. We felt that a good many of them were girlfriends of prisoners and many of them had families, meeting every train in hopes of seeing someone they might know. We felt these little Filipino gatherings where we unloaded off the train were extremely friendly gatherings. People were trying to look for someone or see how we were doing in general. We walked through the streets and saw the sights of Manila. In a way, even though we were prisoners and the guards were escorting us, in many ways I felt like I was in a parade because the Filipinos were excited to see us. They lined the streets like we were a parade. We felt not only were they lining the street to watch us, but they were enthusiastic, sympathetic and concerned about us, and glad to see some of us still alive. We passed several places where we could hear music. The Philippines were beautiful, or it was in those days to me, the colors, smells, and sounds. I really loved it and thought they were great. We would hear the music coming from the little old shops and every so often would hear somebody playing "Auld Lang Syne." We had the idea they were trying to tell us they were with us, they loved us, they knew these days would not go on forever. The Americans were going to win the war and these hated Japanese will be thrown out like they should be. Anyway, we marched through Manila to Bilibid Prison, and I thought it was a thrilling happening. It would be an intriguing experience to be incarcerated in a territorial prison, a real prison. To think I was going to be able to live inside a real, honest to goodness prison even though at this time it was holding prisoners of war. A notable side light to this is that today, some people have gone back and visited old Bilibid Prison. I've seen some pictures that were enlightening. They are so friendly at the prison today. They invited these ex-prisoners, who had lived in Bilibid, to come inside and look around. They even went to their old rooms where they stayed. They said the current prisoners gathered around and seemed as excited as anybody else that these guys were old inmates and had actually slept in those rooms. They seemed at least as excited as the guards in showing them around. I thought that was really unique that today's prisoners, even though in their sad life, for whatever reason they got into prison, they themselves were interested in the past and interested in our guys who had lived there during the war.

At Bilibid, the food was better. They had organized kitchens. I slept in one of the taller buildings. I guess it was about three stories. It was a fun thing after sleeping on the ground and the bamboo slats. All we did was lay down on concrete, but it was indoors with real windows and all that kind of thing. We felt like we were downtown in a nice place for a change. I was excited to be in Bilibid. I don't know how long I was there, but it was a relatively short period. They issued each of us a T-shirt and one of these large "hands" of tobacco, which was kind of unique. I didn't know what to do with it because I didn't smoke. Everybody had a hand of tobacco so it was not exactly exciting trading material. I carried it with me for quite a while. I don't remember what I did with it. I'm sure that somewhere along the line I gave it to someone. I thought it was fun, carrying around a big bunch of tobacco.

I believe it was close to the 14th or 15th of July when we were taken out and put on a freighter in the middle of Manila's harbor. The pier we left from was the same pier our ship had used when I came in on the *Coolidge* from the United States. This is July and I arrived in the Philippines in November, so I'm guessing two and a half years ago. They called the freighter the *Mati Mati Maru*. I understand it was built by the Canadians back in about 1914, but it had been a Japanese ship for many years. They bought it surplus from the Canadians. Here we were, out on this ship and the water was beautiful; we're having another new experience. We'd been living out there in the center of Luzon all this time, and here was all this water and waves and colorful things. More exciting than that was the approximately 60 Japanese Navy fighting ships of various types in the harbor. It was just unbelievable. They were bobbing in the bay. As far as I could see, there were only ships—war ships, aircraft carriers, everything. I couldn't believe it. There were Japanese going ashore, going from ship to ship, in all these little launches. They were scooting along in the water, loaded with sailors in their white suits. You just can't imagine. The picture was fantastic. It was like standing beside the soldier in his normal uniform, being able to see him close up. Like I talked about when we were in Bataan, when they were firing on Corregidor, here I was again, seeing the Navy the same way. To sit right in the middle of a Navy and, as it turned out, within a month or two this Navy was going to meet Halsey in the southern Philippines, and a bigger part of them were going to be sunk. Of course, we couldn't know that then. We were sitting in the harbor. We weren't out on deck often, but at the time we were on deck for some reason. In fact, the only way to go to the bathroom was going on deck. Suddenly, there was an enormous explosion and a ship blew up right before our eyes. It was some kind of a freighter and it had oil barrels on deck, and the barrels were being blown into the air. The harbor got excited. All the ships started scurrying around, going everywhere. I suppose there must have been a submarine there in the harbor, at least they thought there was, so everybody was scooting around to be sure they weren't going to be hit, too. Imagine the excitement with all these ships suddenly getting under way and going in all directions. They had our bathroom places built where they hung over the side of the deck, and it was hard for us to get up there. They were very particular when they were going to let us go on deck to go to the bathroom, which created a problem. Down in the holds, we didn't have a lot of room. At this time, we joined approximately the same amount of people from the south who'd come up from the southern islands. We had approximately 1,000 prisoners on the boat. While we were still in the harbor, they gave us some soup, rice and shrimp, all cooked together, which might have been one of the tastier meals we had. We didn't get much soup, mainly ricey water, but it was different. Certainly I hadn't seen any shrimp cooked that way before and it was unique.

In a day or two we were under way and we started north out of the harbor at Manila. This freighter we were on was empty except for prisoners. We had our hold down a little ladder, 15 or 20 feet. It was where we would all sleep. There were cubicles, three high, that went all around the outside. It was like crawling under a dining room table. I slept at deck level with two groups sleeping right above me. We were so crowded in there that when we'd lay down, if one turned over, everyone had to turn over. For some reason, they had put straw in those up above us. When they would move around in the straw, the chaff would sift down on us. It was so hot in the hold that everyone wore only their G-strings. The chaff would sift down and we felt terribly itchy and uncomfortable. We all had life preservers, but I don't know whether it would have been any good or not. We slept on our life preservers because they had a small amount of cushioning effect to them. When you'd turn one of them over, they would be black with bed bugs. At night, they would roll canvas over the top of the hold and then it would really get hot. Nobody could go up or down during the night. You were in a miserable situation in these holds.

We started towards Formosa. They brought some pork along but soon it smelled bad. I don't think they had any way to preserve it. It wasn't too long before everybody smelled like pork; the whole ship smelled the same. I don't think anybody was unhappy when it was gone and that wasn't very long. It was just a little seasoning in the rice anyway. The rest of the trip, I believe it was 62 days, we got one little cup of rice and one small cup of water each day. We'd get that at 11:00 every morning. We not only got dirty, our mess kit got dirty, everything was dirty, so I'd pour this little cup of water in my mess kit, wash my mess kit, wash my hands, and then drink the water. A terrible situation, but it was the only effective, efficient way to operate. We had to try to keep our hands clean, and the kit clean, and we certainly couldn't waste a drop of water.

Chapter Twelve

THE TRIP TO JAPAN ON ONE OF THE HELL SHIPS OF THE SUMMER OF 1944

We hadn't left Manila very long when we ran into a typhoon. If I'd known how many ships are lost at sea and how many ships turn over in high waves, I would have been terrorized by what this ship went through. I'd never seen anything like it and hope to never again. We would wallow in the most tremendous waves you can imagine. It's hard for me to imagine, but it appeared the wave ahead of us was maybe 50 feet higher than the ship. As the ship would wallow in the water, it pitched up and then down. In most cases, we didn't actually go through the waves. They kept us below deck and we got very little chance to look at this, especially when it was at its worst. As the ship went down the wave, there would be a huge trough and the ship would stand on its nose in the trough. It wallowed through this trough and as it nosed down, the screws would come out of the water and a horrible vibration would set up. Soon, as the nose (bow) started to rise, it would stand on its rear end (stern) with the nose up in the air. I can't imagine how ships survived in water like that. I wonder if we weren't in danger of turning over at almost any time because we were empty of cargo. It was one of the wildest rides you can imagine. We were probably lucky we were empty. We arrived in Formosa at Takao Harbor and it was like Venice, Italy in a way. We could see streets up this way and streets up that way that were waterways. We pulled alongside a dock and I had an incredible feeling. It was like we were in China. We would see sampans and boats the Chinese use and of course, we were in a part of China. Formosa is part of China. It certainly looked like China. That was a real experience. I don't know how long we were tied up there. One day they allowed us to go ashore. They took water hoses and sprayed water on us so we could wash down, which was a new experience. After a short period at Takao, we went to sea again, around to the north end of Formosa. It was an interesting harbor. I believe it is near Taipei. We slipped into a harbor and as we steamed by, we got to see this place. They had tunnels in the mountains on both sides and railroad tracks so they would wheel guns in and out to fire for their harbor defense. We went down to where there was a small city. We were there for about two weeks. Finally, we cleared the harbor and just as we were leaving the harbor there was a great high mound. You wouldn't call it a hill. You wouldn't call it a mountain. It was just a thousand foot high pillar sticking out of the water right at the harbor entrance. It was an interesting sight. When we cleared that point, we were in open sea again, wallowing along in the water. There were 27 ships in our convoy including some destroyers. We were just out of sight of Formosa when the Japanese started running around hollering, "Submarine, submarine!" The destroyers came scooting alongside the ships and were throwing depth charges out and our ship started zig zagging. It was exciting. In the meantime, the POWs fired up the furnaces of our ship, the *Mata Mata Maru*. We had a terrible time. We would try to get up a little speed and the boilers would blow out. We had eight boilers and it was standard for four of them to go out of commission at one time. With all the excitement happening and everybody clipping along about as fast as they could go, we blew four of our boilers so the whole convoy went off and left us. We wallered around and went into Okinawa. If there were submarines out there, they either left or got sunk or maybe they weren't really there. Maybe the Japanese just got excited. It was quite an exciting period for us. We arrived in Okinawa and I consider this one of my best experiences. We got a pretty good view of the land as we went down the coast after we took on a load of salt. We could see the farmers and people on the roads. It was a homey exciting feeling to move along the coastline and see these things. We tied up at Okinawa and were there for about four days. As we were preparing to leave, we saw two good-sized ships and they were being loaded with civilian men. All day long they loaded civilians. The boats kept coming out from the shore. Finally, we were ready to go, everybody was getting up steam and the ships were beginning to jockey around like they do at times. We were trying to get our anchor up. The steam outfit that raised the anchor was chugging and grinding and chunking and the chain was banging and clanging. Boy, if you've never seen one of these enormous anchor chains, they were something else. With all the chugging, jerking, jumping, and trying to get our anchor up, we couldn't leave and so the ships sailed off without us. Historically, what happened was the ships left (there was even a movie made about it), were caught by the Americans and sunk the next day. So, it was lucky thing we couldn't get our anchor up. I lived such a charmed life as a prisoner all those times when I should have died and didn't, God's blessing I presume. I lived and this happened again and again. So after a day or two, we finally tried again and got our anchor up and sailed on into Japan. No sweat. Nobody bothered us, just chunked along through the sea. We were living over a load of salt and could lift the boards up underneath us and we could look down in the hold. It looked like a sea of salt underneath us. In fact, the salt was so close you could jump down into it and with a little help, the guys climbed back out again. As we came into Japan, we sailed by all sorts of little islands at night and for some reason, we were able to be up and see, which was kind of unusual. It was interesting to look out and be slipping along through the water, seeing the waves being cut through in the moonlight, looking over the side and seeing all these islands and lights here and there. You wonder what all of these people are doing and what all the lights are about. It was another exciting experience for me. We finally landed in Moji, Japan. I understood it's a good-sized town and it's quite a seaport. We pulled in and unloaded. We were divided up and sent to different camps. There was a lot going on in that harbor the day we landed. A bunch of ships were loading soldiers to go to the war. This was September of 1944, and the war was going pretty bad for them. I'm sure it was depressing, with all these soldiers having to go to war and all the people down there to see them off. It caused a tense situation in the area. They were lining us up and one of the Japanese came up. He looked the same, wrapped leggings, little old cap, and he was just another "Jap" to us and he says, "Okay, you guys, line up over there. Don't try to give me any of your bull. I know what you're thinking. I went to high school in Riverside, California so just be careful and keep yourself out of trouble." It shocked us. Here he's talking like an American and yet he looks like one of them. We lined up, sat around, they fed us something and we stayed under a little tin shed for the day. We took in the sights and sounds of the harbor. It was, again compared to sitting or working in prison camp every day, nice to see something new and different again. About dark, they marched us over to a train and it looked as though the people were not terribly happy. They were losing the war, all their soldiers were leaving, and I suppose seeing us made them pretty unhappy with us. I sort of felt a comradeship with the guards there. I was glad they were there. They got us up and on the train and pulled the curtains down. We were crowded on the train. I found that because the seats were so high, I could crawl under one of the seats and go to sleep. It was night and I just crawled down under a seat, made myself a bed and went to sleep. I slept all night. A lot of the guys were pretty tired. We arrived the next morning at about 4:00 A.M. It was almost light as we pulled into this train station. There were lights around the station. They opened the doors, got us out, lined us up and marched us off to our new camp. They marched us into Camp 17 at Amuta, another new and exciting experience. We were actually walking through Japan, a nice change, and got to see the place. They had large electrical wires. Everywhere we looked there were these great enormous electric wires and great conductors. I thought, "Gee, Japan must be total electric." This was a good-sized city close to Nagasaki. In fact, it was right in the same bay area. They were loading coal by hand, men and women. They would walk with a bamboo or wood pole over their shoulder with a little basket in front and back. They would squat down and fill these baskets, then put their shoulder under this wood pole and walk over to the train car. They'd walk up a ramp and take their hands and dump their little bundles of coal into the train car. Then they'd go back down and repeat it. As we walked through this coal town, an electric town, an industrial town, it really was something to see. It was a lot more modern than I expected it to be. On the other hand, it was so primitive, watching the people dumping their baskets in the train cars.

POW conditions in hold of hell ship on the way to Japan

Chapter Thirteen

LIFE IN PRISON CAMP 17 IN JAPAN

We arrived at our camp, they opened the front gate and we marched inside the gate. They lined us up so the prisoners who were already there could see us. They were all gathered around looking at these newcomers. We lined up and checked in. We had to give our names and go through this routine. They had an interesting procedure. I can't imagine what the point was, but we had to sign a paper that said we wouldn't try to escape. My thought was, "What in the world difference would a piece of paper make to me stating that I promised not to escape? If I got a chance to escape, I would. Why in the world would they want me to sign a piece of paper saying I wouldn't?" I've talked to German prisoners of war who said they didn't have to work because that was a Geneva Convention rule. Possibly if we signed it, they felt their consciences would be clear in shooting us if we were caught. They would have shot us. They must have felt this technically released them from something. For me to sign that I wouldn't try to escape was just on the edge of ridiculous.

We got checked in and it was fun to be in a new place. They issued us a few things we hadn't had in the past. They issued us a pair of split toed tennis shoes, something that I wished I had brought back to the States with me. They issued us what they called a mine uniform. It was a burlap bag dyed green, sort of a sloppy looking suit. So you had a suit coat jacket and a pair of trousers made out of material a lot like a burlap bag, only it was dyed green. That was the only piece of new clothes I had the entire time I was a prisoner, and the only thing in the way of trousers I was ever issued, except when we were issued a used Japanese uniform. It included the knee pants, the shirt and a cap. So I had a cap, shirt, and a pair of pants just like the Japanese soldier. To this day, I wish I had brought them home. I've never seen anybody with one so I guess nobody brought theirs home. It would have been a lot of fun to show around. We were now prepared to begin our new life at Camp 17 Amuta. It was a lot more organized and clean. They also issued each of us two nice new-looking comforters. This was really something. Wow, we hadn't had anything like it. We also got one very hard pillow. In Japan, they use pillows made out of something similar to what a broom is made of. It was woven into a thing that you could put your head on and call it a pillow if you liked.

We were assigned to our area. We were called the new Americans and were assigned numbers. My number was 1260. I believe approximately 200 of us came to this camp at this time. Our numbers ran from in the low 1100s to the low 1300s. So we had guys who were number 1100, 1136, and then we had guys numbered 1305. That totals out to about 200, I believe. We were assigned to barracks number 20 and 21 shotai. We got nice rooms that held 12 to 13 people. Again, it was a new experience to be in a room with a floor-like matting. There were doors that slid open into the room and paper was pasted on the back of them. I had always heard about the Japanese and their paper doors and paper windows. We were all set up for a new experience in these barracks. There was a row of rooms down the side hall into the back. Also, we had a bathroom right in our building. We had a place to go, like a commode. It wasn't a commode, just an outhouse attached to the building. We had a pegboard outside of our room and on the pegboard everybody would hang their number. If you were in the room, your number hung on the "in room" line. If you were at work you moved your peg down to "at work." If you were eating at the dining room, you'd have it hung there. If you were at the bathroom, there was a place to hang it there. So if you weren't where your tag said you were, you were in big trouble. For example, there were 13 of us in the room. If a guard came by in the night and looked in your door and counted only 12 people, then he would look at the pegboard and see if 12 were in the room. They never turned the light off. There was one big bulb that hung in the middle of the room and kept the whole room bathed in a bright light at all times. I don't recall if it was on during the day. Surely, it was just at night. If one peg was moved down to the bathroom, then he'd go down to the bathroom to see if someone was there. If the count didn't work out, you could bet somebody was going to be beat up. For example, if it said that 13 were in the room and there were only 12 and he went down to the bathroom and one was down in the bathroom, well, the guy in the bathroom was in for a beating. So, any time we weren't where we were supposed to be, or if one of us went to the bathroom and left the tag on "bathroom" and came back and laid down and went to sleep, the guard would come, find the number and call out that number, then call you out and beat you. You were going to get a beating if you weren't where you were supposed to be. Otherwise, these barracks were pretty nice. They were certainly newer than what we'd been in before. We enjoyed the new comforters, which was something different for us after living so primitively and all the dying that went on. We felt like we were in a new world. To some extent, it wasn't a terrible place, but then on the other hand, it wasn't a good place by any stretch of the imagination. It's not a place any of you would ever want to see. There were a considerable number of people who died in this camp, but not anything like the deaths of the early days. I guess probably 10 to 15% of this camp died. Deathwise, it was much lower than what we've talked about at O'Donnell and Cabanatuan. For the Americans, this was a coal mine camp. In the end, we had approximately 1,700 prisoners. There were the Australians, British, Dutch, what were called the new Americans and the people who opened the camp. I believe there were 500 of the old Americans and about 200 of us new Americans.

In the dining hall in Camp 17 where 1700 people ate all hours of the day, food was bought and sold almost constantly. There were always people buying and selling food, just like at a stock market. People would be offering rice for 2 ½ yen while someone else would be saying, "I'll pay 2 yen for rice," or "I have soup for 75 sen," and another would say, "I am buying soup at 50 sen." If someone came back from the dining hall you would ask, "How's the meal?" He might say, "Rice is going for 2 yen and soup is going for 75 sen," depending on supply and demand and to some extent the quality of the soup. So one would feel like he was in a marketplace plus, of course, you're dealing with four nationalities: the Americans, the Dutch, the Aussies, and the British. Some people would play the market as a racket, manipulating the price by taking low bids, then waiting for the market to rise and sell it higher. People were able to do this by studying other people's habits and needs.

The Americans, Australians and Dutch worked in the coal mines. The British worked in a zinc factory. Although the coal mine was hell in many ways, I'm glad we worked there instead of the zinc factories, because they fired the furnaces and the story of that is pretty horrible. The British who worked there looked horrible. Their skin was browned or scorched with something because they fed these furnaces with temperatures up to 3,500 degrees. They'd feed coal into these furnaces. As I recall, the British would tell us they'd shovel for 15 minutes and jump in a water tank for about 15 minutes to cool off. In the coal mine, we worked in three complete shifts. The work was endless. There was no change in the schedule. That meant we had eight hours of working plus we had time tacked onto the end of our shifts to make up for when we had lined up, marched over, got organized, and went down into the mines. We had to relieve the other guys just as they were coming off their shift. This added an hour or two on the end of each shift so it ended up we were gone at our job from 10 to 12 hours. The shifts in the mine were continuous. We were lined up inside the camp, counted off, and marched to the mine. The mine had big buildings where there were workshops and people working around the mine. We would go over into the actual mine area where the entrance trains were and we'd be lined up again. There was a great enormous statue of Buddha. We were required to bow to the statue each day before getting on the train to go down. We didn't know what we were supposed to say, but we were to take off our hats and all bow at the same time. It sounded like they said, "Hats off." We would take our hats off, bow and say, "Hats off." This seemed to work just fine. When we got this routine out of the way, we'd all catch our train. The entrance to the mine was slanted at an angle that appeared to be in the neighborhood of 45 degrees, however, it was probably not quite that steep. This is where the trains would go down. As you looked down into the mine, you'd see the track leading off on an inclined plane. Since the mine was under the ocean, it was pointed down that way. When we were at the bottom of the shaft, we could look back up and see a tiny pin point of light that was the outside. It was an enormous entrance, 75 feet high. It was a long way up to the top and a long ways down. Anyway, we'd get on the trains and down into the mine we'd go. We normally worked on Dia

Roku, which meant level six. We'd get down to the bottom, unload from the trains, and go to our various work stations. I was normally assigned to wall and roof bracing which was the preparation part of the work. The last shift had been the coal shovelers. Now we were the workers who would reconstruct and build the braces against the ceiling, brace up the wall where it had been dug out. The next crew that would come in would be the dynamite crew in my area. It was rotated in the various areas. The crew that followed my particular shift was the dynamite crew. They would come in and drill into the coal face. Normally, they would drill 125 holes. After they got all the holes drilled, they would put dynamite in the holes and as their day ended they would blow all the coal face down. When they left, the shoveling crew would come in and they would spend their shift shoveling the coal into the troughs and carrying the coal away. I worked down there for a year. In fact, I hadn't much more than started work in the mine until I was having considerable trouble. It was determined I had a hernia. I saw the Japanese mine doctor and was sent to the American doctors and they decided to operate. I was operated on by Dr. Hewlett and as I learned later, the operation was carried out with the use of a little bit of novocaine. They'd take a small amount of spinal fluid out, mix it with a little dental novocaine, and then re-inject it into the spine. A doctor, who will remain unnamed for this story, was on the boat with me and when I first showed him my hernia, he said I had an internal infection. He said that I should lay down a lot, which of course was no help. It wasn't an infection and I was sure it wasn't at the time. I knew I had been ruptured lifting heavy loads in Cabanatuan. When I saw Dr. Hewlett in Camp 17, he said I had a hernia, even though the doctor I just mentioned insisted I still had an infection. He said to Dr. Hewlett, "Well, he doesn't have the proper symptoms." Dr. Hewlett said, "Oh, he certainly does. The symptoms he has are very common." One time I was over in the hospital and got an idea of how incompetent the rest of the doctors felt this particular doctor was. One of the sergeants came running over from the sick call clinic at top speed and burst into the room and said, "One of you doctors better get over there. He's got a sick man. He'll kill him." He'd had a guy in from the mine with a broken jaw. They were pushing a coal car back into a dead end and he'd gotten his jaw caught between one of these ceiling brace poles and the railroad car. In any case, that gave me a good idea what they thought of this particular gentleman as a doctor. So, I was in there waiting on the table for my operation. They had done everything they were going to. A couple of corpsmen were holding me and about that time this doctor who we had very little respect for walked into the room. I said, "You're not going to operate on me are you?" He said, "No, Dr. Hewlett is going to." God looked after me again. I was operated on and after my operation my doctor was thrown in the guardhouse. He was talking to the Japanese guards about how soon the people could go back to work. They got mad and threw him in the guardhouse. Since my surgeon was locked up, he wasn't able to come in and check on me. I got an infection in my wound. It swelled up and broke open. About the time the doctor got out of the guardhouse, which was nearly 20 days after my operation, he came into the room and he looked at my incision and he said, "Oh, my God." He got a pair of scissors, wrapped some gauze around it, reached up and drug those scissors right down through the center of it. From then on I got better; the thing healed pretty good as far as I could tell and I went back to work in the coal mine. I was now one of the regular coal mine workers.

In the mines we worked pretty hard. After I went back, they decided I should work light duty. They put me on the jack hammer crew. That was the reason I learned so much about the jack hammer. We drilled holes in the coal face and blew it down. I worked with them for maybe two months. It was rather interesting. I enjoyed drilling the holes and blowing the coal face down. The jack hammer wasn't all that hard of a job. The straight in shot was easy. The down shot was easy. The only one that was really difficult was the up shot. One third of them had the up shots where you would have to hold the jack hammer kind of on your chest and push it up at about a 45 degree angle. That was difficult. I enjoyed my time on the dynamite crew, too. I was eventually sent back to my regular shift with the rest of the guys. I look back on the mine experiences as maybe quite a bit of fun, although it was intermittent with beatings and mistreatment. We had some pretty funny and not so funny things go on from time to time. One time, we were in a dead end working. We weren't on Dia Roku (level six) at that time, we were on Diasan, level three. That was the only time I worked up there. I don't really know why I was sent there. We were working a dead end and there were no Japanese we knew. One was a mean rascal and was always chewing on us. They told us to take our loaded coal car way back in the tunnel. We were to take our light off our hat and flash it, then a man would pull our coal car back up and dump it. Then he'd run down another car down. So we had our coal car about full and we saw this rascal. He was drilling with a power hammer and had drug his air hoses across the railroad track. We thought, oh boy, this is our chance. So we flashed our light and before he could get his hoses back across, the train had run over his hoses and cut them. You never heard so much screaming and yelling and carrying on in your life. Fortunately, he thought we were too dumb to know what we had done and didn't waste his time coming down and beating on us. This was rather unusual, because under most circumstances in a deal like that we would have been in for a real good beating.

Normally, we worked what we called "walk-a-bys," bracing the ceiling. The ceilings would vary all the way from 10 feet to maybe 20 feet high. Our job was to get logs and build a log cabin structure, filling these structures with rocks clear to the ceiling. As we built the structures and braced the logs, we'd take additional rocks and block in the side until we had a solid foundation. However, they didn't furnish us the logs we needed. Our next choice was to use whatever rocks we could find. There weren't many rocks available of the kind we needed to brace the ceiling. It's kind of like being in the Army. They tell you what needs to be done, but don't give you what you need to do it with. In any case, we had limited choices but we did have to construct a wall up there. The simplest thing for us to do was to go four or five days back and just pull the logs out from where they'd been before. We'd pull those logs out that had been used three, four, five shifts ago, bring them forward and build our new wall. It wasn't very safe under those big cut outs of coal, the whole thing is in one great big square. The only thing holding those things up is the walls that we built. There were some pretty lively cave-ins going on back there behind us. That wasn't our problem. Our problem was to get a wall up that day. We'd bring these logs out and pile rocks up behind them. We ran into more problems because we had to get it done, had limited time, and we had to build with something. If there weren't rocks available, what in the world could we use? We ended up throwing coal back into the walk-a-bys to get them filled. Sometimes our own personal bosses who were in charge of that particular wall would even encourage us to do that. Sometimes we'd be shoveling coal and if one of the bosses came along, he'd be watching and would holler at us to make us quit and act like he was real incensed that we were putting coal in the wall. He was actually encouraging us because he was just like us. He had to get a job done, so many times he didn't care. We'd do various things such as put rocks back there at a slant so the hole would fill up quicker and then fill it with more coal. Some of the guys would take big engines used to pump water down there and put them inside the walls. When the Japanese were trying to figure out their inventory, they would become pretty discouraged when they were looking for a $5,000 engine and couldn't find it because it was buried back there in one of those walls.

There was one Jap we worked for we called "slope head," "no good son of a gun," "dumb jerk," and "rice patty jerk." We'd make all kinds of little remarks. He didn't speak any English and we were always getting beat up. He was a mean old rascal. People hated to work for him because he was so mean. One time, we were talking with one of the "old" Americans and we said, "Wacki san doesn't understand any English." "He doesn't? Wait a minute." He went up to him and said, "Hey, Wacki san, what time is it?" Wacki san answered, "Oh, about 4:45." Then we knew why we got all those beatings.

The work got intolerable in the mine. We were on limited rations and many of the men felt they were going to die in the mine because the work was too hard and they didn't have enough vitamins or energy. They were too run down. It was just a matter of time before we'd die working down there. Many of the men began making plans to break their arms and legs. If you could break an arm or have somebody break it for you, then you could get a month or so topside where you had a chance to get by on the rations that were available and have light duty. There got to be a real business going in broken arms. I had a friend named Mason and he decided to break his leg. He got a guy to help him and they were going to use a railroad iron to break the leg. They were beating on his leg with this railroad iron and it wouldn't break. Mason was talking to me afterwards and said, "Hamilton, whatever you do, don't try to break your leg." It actually worked out for him, though. He beat up his leg so bad it got infected and he got a lot more time off than if he had broken his leg. He was out with this bad leg for a long time.

An incident happened to me. I was working in an area, I forget exactly what it was, but I was off of the main lateral. All of a sudden there was a cave-in and I got hit on top of the head with a rock. We had padded caps on top of our heads and a light on the front, and we wore a battery around our belt. That's about all we wore. We wore a G-string, a belt, a cap, and sometimes shoes. Many times the guys just worked barefooted, but sometimes we wore these little split-toed tennis shoes. Anyway, there was a cave-in and a large rock fell on my head. Even with this padded cap, I took a blow on top of the head that split my head right down the center. The skin broke open, blood ran down my hair, both sides of my head, down my forehead, and down the back of my head. After you've been in the coal mine for a little while, you're all covered with coal dust. I was just black with coal dust when this blood ran down through my hair and all over me. The minute my boss saw me he said, "Go up to the tool shack and lay down." I suppose he thought I was brained and would die. I didn't feel like I was really hurt that bad and as it turned out, I wasn't. It just split the skin on top of my head; there was a lot of blood but I didn't seem to be seriously hurt. I went up to the tool shack and some Jap would come along and he'd think he had caught an American loafing. He would see me over there on the bench, roll me over and look at the blood all over me, give a little disgusted and disappointed grunt and leave me alone. I had it pretty good, loafing that day. When I got topside, they took me to a clinic that had nurses, washed my head off, put some kind of antiseptic on it and put a few stitches in the top of my head.

I spent a year working in the mine. I missed time for my surgery and one time I had chicken pox. A lot of exciting things happened. Some of them were fun things. I kind of enjoyed working in the mines. In January, I got chicken pox.

I felt terrible. I went to the mine for a couple days with it and I couldn't believe how sick I was. I was so sick I didn't know what to do. I couldn't figure out why and didn't know whether I should go to sick call or not, so I went on down in the mine. About the third day, I noticed I was breaking out with little water blisters. I wondered what it was. I came in from my late shift that night and went to the doctor. He looked at my blisters and said, "Boy, are you lucky. You've got chicken pox." He was right. They had one barracks over there that they set aside for the chicken pox. The Japanese agreed with them that chicken pox was a highly contagious disease and the people ought to be isolated. I was in isolation and man, I had the nicest old bed. We had a great big bowl like a big wok where we could take our baths, a personal bath in our own building. Everyone who had chicken pox was left alone in there and as long as you had three scabs you didn't have to go back to duty. I stretched that into three weeks. It was probably the best three weeks of my whole prison life. I had a nice sunny window and I could look out at the guys going to the mine, but eventually I had to go back to work.

A lot of exciting and interesting things happened down in the mine. It was kind of a fun time in my prison life as far as experiences go. We'd do all kinds of things. One time we were breaking up rocks and building walls with regular jack hammers. We also had what we called stofers. They were big jack hammers. They stretched from the floor to the ceiling. Boy, they were enormous hammers and they made a racket. It's no wonder I have poor hearing these days, because in that mine you just couldn't believe the noise. I might refer to *Dante's Inferno* again because so many things remind me of it. Here we were, with maybe 20 to 30 foot ceilings in some places. Along the wall, maybe it's only 15 to 16 feet because when they blew it down, there were more blows down in the center than along the side. Maybe three guys are working the regular jack hammer and maybe two are working the stofer.

The rest of the guys are dragging logs and we are all covered with coal dust. We're black from head to toe wearing G-strings, and there's no central light. We've all got our personal lights. It's a picture you just have to see to have any idea at all what it looked like. Anyway, this guy was working this big jack hammer, floor to ceiling, and I was trying to build a wall and he got me irritated. He's running that big hammer and every little bit he'd stop and blow dust all over me. I got so irritated at that guy I said, "Get that darn hammer out of here." I practically threatened him. He looked upset and took his hammer and moved it down a little farther. I'll be darned if in five minutes, right where he'd been standing, enough rock fell in there to kill him twice. I saved the guy's life but I don't think he really understood or cared. It was just one of those things that happened when you're working.

Another incident happened similar to that one. One night, we'd worked hard and finally the whistle called to go and we all started to leave. We walked to where we turned off into the side tunnel to leave the shaft we were working in. We had just left the shaft and I couldn't believe it, but everything caved in. We turned around and looked back and that place was absolutely filled with rock. If we had been in the shaft five more minutes, I don't think a single one of us would have lived. The dust rose up from the cave-in and we stood there in disbelief. Many times the rocks would fall like that. The rocks were like a white granite. We worked in our G-strings with our bare backs exposed. One could tell if there might be a cave-in coming because if we could feel sand sifting down on our backs, that was a pretty good indication rocks were moving and grinding off their edges. In just a little bit, something was going to drop and we had better move.

One night we were in a tunnel and it was really braced up. They had engineers working for them. Somebody knew what was going on. It was a pretty complicated mine. In this particular area, it was braced up good. You couldn't believe the size of the logs they had holding that ceiling up. Man, some of those logs must have been 14 inches across. They were thick, like one every five or six feet. One night we were working and all of a sudden one of the Japs hollered, "Miya" which means go. "Miya" he yelled, ducked down, grabbed his pick and started running. So we started running too. I just couldn't believe it, but that ceiling started coming down just like a giant press. Those logs would go "pop" and break into slivers. They would tear and split apart because there was so much weight being pressed down on them that they disintegrated under the weight. I couldn't believe it. Don't think we didn't "miya". I mean we miyaed (ran). We tore out of the tunnel as fast as we could go. As it turned out after it dropped several feet, it stopped and we were able to go back in and clean up the mess. It was exciting when we ran out of that one.

One of the bosses told me, "Roku Ju." That was 60, short for my number, 1260. He says, "Bring me a six foot log". I went out, looked for a six foot log and picked out one that looked like it was six foot to me. I brought it back and he measured it. He wanted a six foot log. The one I brought back was about 5 foot 10 inches or so and didn't reach the ceiling. I'll tell you, talk about being mad. That guy started whipping me with his saw. I thought he was going to kill me. Those were the funny kinds of things that happened. He said six foot and you thought he wanted "about" six feet. He didn't want about anything, he wanted six feet.

We had another guy, I can't remember his name, he was a Navy guy. He had a terrible time. He had this great idea that he was going to break his foot. He tried to break it and only made it sore. I mean it was a mess and he hadn't broken anything. We had a big air lock door down in the mines. If you didn't watch it, there would be a change in the air draft and one of those air lock doors would jerk shut; it would just about kill you if you got caught in it. He thought, well that's where he could break his foot. So he got in one of those air lock doors and the thing slammed shut on his foot. I tell you, the poor guy, was in all kinds of pain. Can you believe, when they x-rayed it, it still wasn't broken.

We had a Japanese supervisor guard named Beetle. That rascal, I tell you he was some kind of mean. He beat up on everybody. One of the things he liked best was he just loved to catch somebody doing something wrong. We had to step across these conveyor belts when we were carrying something and there was a great big chain running down the center. If you'd fall on that chain, man, it would tear you to pieces. It was a dangerous thing to be stepping over, let alone falling in. Sometimes we'd have to carry 12 foot logs on our shoulders. We weren't very strong, so we were trying to balance this log on our shoulders. We got pretty good at balancing these logs. We would get half on one side and half on the other and get it up on our shoulders. We were right in the center and it's balanced and you walk with it. It's hard to walk on that uneven ground and now you have to step across this conveyor belt. One of Beetle's favorite tricks was to catch a guy just as he stepped across that belt and kick him in the rear end. It was quite unnerving. You began to drop your end of the log and scramble for your life so you wouldn't get tore up in this belt. Beetle wasn't the most popular man in the mine. In fact, a good many of us hated the guy. We had these great big things in the ceiling that looked like black glass, a black material they make insulators out of for telephone poles. It looked like solid stone and ebony in color. They came in big bunches, maybe a ton of them, right in with the coal. When you came to one of those things overhead, they were subject to falling out at any time. You want to dig them out so they won't fall on somebody. One night, Beetle was trying to dig one out with his pick. He was digging around the edges and darn if that thing didn't fall on him and kill him. I tell you, the word went through the mine like lightning. In minutes, everyone working in the mine knew Beetle was dead. The guards wanted us to get in trouble. They were all upset because they knew the prisoners were happy because Beetle was dead. They came through and said, "Beetle's dead. Is that good?" and you'd say, "Oh no, that's very bad. Most unfortunate." But we were tickled to death we were through with darned old Beetle. We lived with people that beat on us constantly and worked us as slave labor. They cared so little for our welfare, you eventually got the idea that the only good ones were dead ones. It is not a good thought, but you can understand how it ends up that way.

In the mines, the supervisor wore different lights. The prisoners wore a white light. If he had a little red curlicue in the white light, he was a supervisor or a guard. If he was important, he had a stripe across his light. He was more important if he had two stripes across his light, if he was a two striper. If he was really a big guy, he was a three striper. When we saw somebody coming and they had stripes on their light, we would step lively because this guy was running the show. One night a two-striper came and caught me shoveling coal into the wall basement. He said, "Conei" and I knew what he meant right away. "You're shoveling coal in that thing. What do you think you're doing?" I said, "Wakarimasen," and that means "I don't know what you're talking about." He was so mad, he whipped on me a couple of times with his cane and said, "Conei" (coal) and I said, "Wakarimasen" (I don't understand). So, I figured my best bet was not to try to explain my shoveling coal into the wall. The only thing for me to do was to pretend that I didn't know what he was saying. After he whipped on me a bit with his cane, he finally gave up, cussed me some more, and left. I thought I was really in trouble, getting caught shoveling coal into our wall.

We had other things happen. Screamer was a guy who had been there probably as long as anybody. He was a Japanese

127

supervisor. In a way, he was a halfway nice guy, but he was bad, too. Nobody was really good, but some of them weren't as bad as others. Some of the guys liked Screamer. In fact, he'd been there so long the old Americans knew him and had a pretty good thing going with him. Screamer knew me, too, since I'd worked with him for quite a while. He'd holler, "Roko Ju" (60), the last two numbers on my number 1260. One night we were working with another boss called Saki San. We were working on one wall and some other guys were working on another wall with the Screamer. Screamer came over, looked at our wall, and we hadn't filled it clear to the ceiling. There was a little bit of space left to the ceiling where it could have been filled in with something. He called me over to him and said, "Roko Ju" (ceiling). "Put it all the way to the ceiling. Get it right." I said, "Hai" (Yes). So, I went over and talked to the other guys. "The Screamer says this isn't high enough. We've got to go clear to the ceiling." The guys said the hell with the Screamer. The Screamer started dozing and we started to walk off without finishing. He woke up, saw it and said, "Roko Ju Koi. Come here." So, I went over and he put the whip on me because we didn't build it to the ceiling. I thought that was kind of funny at the time.

The night the B-29s came over and bombed us and the lights went out, Saki san called me over and said, "Denki Nai" which means no electricity. He whipped on me but it was worth it. The tunnels we traveled through were many times very low and we would have to stoop over to go through them. We were working in just our G strings so our bare backs scraped the logs above us. It kept a constant scab on my back. The guards would hassle us, too. They would be running along behind us and if we slowed down, they would jab us in the rear end with a pick handle. If it hadn't been so pathetic it would have been funny.

One time we went in one of the tunnels with the low ceiling and there was an engine back in there. It was wet, the logs were broken over, water was dripping from the ceiling, it was a real mess. We could barely see that silly engine. It was a big one and the boss told us we should get that engine out. Here's a bunch of GIs looking at it who said, "You can't get that out with seven cranes." Boy, I'll tell you, those Japanese figured that one out. They had some ropes brought in. We got the ropes on the engine, then got a hold and put rollers under it and then we'd say, "Sole he kay." Every time we'd say, "Kay" we'd jerk. It wasn't any time until that engine came snaking out of there. There wasn't a soul there when we first looked at that engine and thought we'd never get it out. They were very ingenious fellows. The Japanese were hard workers and strong and knew what they were doing. They'd lived in mines all their lives, so maybe I'm giving them more credit than they deserve. It was under the ocean and there was a lot of dripping water in that ceiling. There was so much dripping that many times the water would be running by where we were working, like a river. They had great enormous pumps in the bottom of the mine that were constantly pumping this water out. Anytime the pumps stopped, the mine started filling with water. It's a strange feeling to be standing in that much water and the water is so cold. It was unbelievably cold. A lot of the guys would get under one of these big drips and wash off before they left the mine. That way they wouldn't be so dirty when they got topside, but the water was so cold if I stepped under it, it would take my breath away. I just couldn't do it very often. There were lots of little fun things we'd do in the mine. There was no central lighting, so the only light in the tunnel was what we had on our caps. If there weren't too many of us around and we wanted it dark, all we had to do was stick our lights down in the coal. We"d see some old lonesome guard wandering around where he didn't have a lot of help and didn't have any light but his own, and we'd bury our lights in the coal and pitch rocks at him. He would have a fit. He would have no idea where the rocks were coming from. He couldn't see us because there wasn't any light.

We had an incident where we were working and we were just about finished when a great big hunk of rock fell like you wouldn't believe. It just fell across from the other side. I suppose it was ten feet high and ten feet across and eight feet thick or something like that. It fell on Johnny Normal, one of our boys, and pinned him and broke his legs. It broke below and above the knees. He was pinned under this enormous rock and we were in there trying to break the rock away so we could get him out and get him topside. That was the night we had one guard. I can't remember his name but he was really a nice guy. I didn't work for him that much but some of the others did. The guards were trying to get Johnny out. They were kind of like us, laughing and making jokes, and here this poor guy's pinned under the rock with both of his legs just shattered. This other guard said to us, "Don't worry. This isn't going to take long. This is just about over and everything's going to be entirely different." He was telling us the war was about to end and we were going to win.

We had just returned to topside and were getting ready to take our baths. We took a bath every night before we went to our barracks. They had a big bath house. We were black with coal dust and if we put our clothes on without washing, it would be horrible. One night the guards told us to go back down in the mine. We went back down into the mine to about the 500 foot level. We could look out and see the great big entrance up above us. We sat down there for I don't know how long, but we'd just sit and feel the lightest little tremor. Finally they said it was all clear and we could come out. We went back topside and most of the mine's shops were blown away. Buddha was gone. That place had really been hit. We were tickled. After that, the Japanese people took what they had left of their shops down to the bottom level and set up offices and everything. It was warm and light down there. and some of those offices were at the sixth level down. They looked so nice, I wondered why they were not there in the first place. Why in the world did they have them up there in that cold topside all the time when they could have been in the nice warmth? When the Americans bombed, they put out the electricity. These big pumps in the bottom of the mines had to keep working to keep it from filling up. We were sent down to the deepest level called the water floor. The water was swirling and boy, it was just pouring in. It was like we were in a big tank with a spigot in the top and it was filling up. There was a whole bunch of equipment they wanted to save down there. They were trying to get the pumps back on, we were wallowing around in water, trying to get a hold of those big engines and slowly they came out. It was funny, almost like a holiday. We got a big kick out of it. We would have loved to see those engines going under water, see them lose their equipment. We'd wallow around, pretend we were struggling and I'll be darned if they didn't bring a great big pan of rice balls down for all the Koreans and the Japs and they didn't give us any. To this day, I think if we had been included in the rice balls, our guys would have probably snaked those engines out for them. But the way it was, they lost almost everything. That was a fun day. We got a kick out of seeing everything ruined. Anything to help the war effort was a good deal. Even though we weren't active soldiers, by golly we were certainly helping our side if we could help the Japanese lose equipment.

One time I was working with another guard and he was a pretty mean guy. His name has slipped my mind. He had me drilling with a jack hammer on a great big rock. It was slippery on this rock. I'd have done fine if he would have left me alone, but he thought he needed to help me. We both had on these little split-toed tennis shoes. He got up on that old

131

slippery rock and pretty soon he fell off. I swear he was so mad. I grabbed the bit and he took it away from me and started flinging it at me. The bit was an inch in diameter and he would have killed me with it if I hadn't grabbed it and held on. I thought, the first time that bit hits me, I'm a dead man. The only thing for me to do was grab the end of it, hang on and see what happens. He was cussing, screaming, kicking and hitting. He was whipping on me and hitting and yelling and screaming. Pretty soon, he stirred up a big crowd of Japanese and all the other prisoners came. He got such a big crowd I guess he decided he couldn't go on and beat me to death in front of everybody. He put the bit down and beat me by hand and that was no problem, I could stand a little of that. I sure didn't want to get killed by that bit. I made a wild gamble that day and it saved my life.

We worked for 10 days and then got a day off. We had the 3rd, 13th, and 23rd off of every month. I've talked enough about the coal mine so I'll just tell you how it all ended.

Back to camp life. Our barracks were numbers 20 and 21, the name of the barracks for the new Americans. We'd have a roll call, we called it "tinko," every night. We'd fall out for roll call in the evening just before supper if that was our shift and we were in camp. People were eating at all times of day because of the three shifts, but everybody who was in camp at tinko time would fall out on the parade ground. A Japanese guard would stand up on a big platform in front, generally a petty officer. He'd have a big sword and a secretary-type person would come along with a clip board. I enjoyed the roll calls. I thought they were unique. I had been in a lot of military formations in the U.S. Army, but I think this was quite interesting. We would line up in columns of twos and by section. We had two sections and there must have been about 100 of us in each section because there were 200 of us in 20 and 21. We would line up in two rows and as the officer conducting the tinko would come down to our section, we'd call out "Nijya Shotai," which was "20 section," or "Nijyuchi shotai," which was "21 section," and they'd say, "Bongo" which meant "count off." Then the front row would count off and he would count down to how many was in the front row. For example, if there were 45 people standing in line in the front row, he'd holler "Yon ju go," which was 45. If the guy in the back row said that was right, he'd holler, "Bon." There was always one more in the front row than there was in the back row if they weren't even. So, if it wasn't even the guy behind would holler "Kisu." So, if the guy would holler 45 in the front row and he hollered bon behind you, you immediately knew there was 90 people standing there, which made it real easy. You could listen to roll call like that without even looking; you could tell what was going on. Then the section chief would holler out how many people were in the hospital, how many people were in the coal mine, or whatever the case might be. So, everybody was counted that way and I enjoyed having a tinko like that. It was so effective and efficient, I thought something like that in our army would be nice.

We also had another nice thing. We had baths that were like indoor swimming pools. They were full of hot water. We would take little buckets and dip out water, soap ourselves, wash ourselves with the little buckets, and all the water would run down the drains. We would wash ourselves good, then get in the main tub and soak in warm water. In this cold place with snow on the ground in the winter, with paper windows and no heat in the buildings, those warm baths really felt good. If I was in camp, I always tried to go to the bath just before we'd have roll calls.

We had a big dining hall where we ate. We were feeding 1,700 people, not all at the same time, but it would hold a lot of people. We had grey clipboards and everybody's number was on the clipboard. They had little golf tees and under each number; there were three little holes. At the beginning

133

of that day, if I came in, they'd put a golf tee in my hole. I had three holes, and when there were three golf tees in my holes that was it, no more eating. I don't suppose too many people lost out, but anyone tricky enough to give the wrong number wouldn't have a meal because of the three golf tees in his holes. That meant you could actually come in most any time of the day or night and as long as you still had an empty hole, you could eat. The menu in camp didn't change at all. They didn't have the old logoa like we had in the Philippines. In Japan they just steamed the rice and whatever they had and made some kind of soup. The soup might be almost nothing or have some dog in it, a little radish or might have a sweet potato vine, even a piece of eggplant, things like that. So you had rice and soup three times a day, it really didn't make much difference. If you ate three times a day, you generally ate exactly the same thing three times. Sometimes the menu might change a little during the day, but there was no special reason for it.

The barracks were nice. There was a big light bulb and we had these nice clean comforters to lay on or over ourselves. To that extent, the little rooms were nice. The guys who smoked had a hard time. There couldn't be any matches, so the only way they could get a light was to go up to the guards to ask them for a light. We had to pay for our cigarettes. We were authorized 10 cigarettes every other day. We got ten "kincies." The guys who smoked would get up in the morning and want to smoke. Mason was in my barracks, it seemed he was always the one who was elected to go for a light, and whoever got the light generally got slapped around for his trouble. He'd have to go through the same silly routine every day. He'd march up to the guard shack, which was up at the end of the street, call himself to attention, salute and tell the guy he needed a light. After a little verbal abuse and a cuff or two, they'd give him a light and he could go on back down to the barracks. That would have been enough encouragement for me to give up smoking right there.

I had an incident that was very scary and my life was saved again by pure chance. It could have been funny, but it wasn't. They say that all humor is tragedy and the pitiful things are the funniest things there are. It seemed like the pitiful things were the things that turned out to be the most humorous. As we would cross the street we were supposed to turn, no matter how far we were down from the guard shack, and face the guard shack, call yourself to attention, call out in a loud voice and salute. You'd say, "keirei," which meant "salute." Then you'd hand salute the guard at the guard shack. One day I was crossing the street for something. I stopped, called right face, attention, called out salute and saluted the guards at the end of the street. They paid no attention to me. Since they were playing cards, I gave myself a left face and started to go on. Just about that time they noticed, and obviously they hadn't noticed me before, so they decided I had not saluted. They yelled at me and called me to the guard shack. They gave me verbal abuse and then took a big club to me that was similar to a baseball bat and hit me across the back. I thought, oh my goodness, if they break my back it will be ruined forever. The funny thing was, I don't even remember my back being sore. They whipped on my back with that big club and kept insisting I hadn't saluted, and I kept insisting I had. The guy asked me if it was okay to go to the guard house and I said yes. If you told them no, you didn't want to go to the guard house, they thought you were a coward. If you were scared to go, you were a goner. The only chance we weren't going was if you could put on enough of a bluff that it was alright with you, you were tough and could take whatever they could give out. He marched me on down towards the guard house. There weren't too many people that came back from the guard house alive. One of their neat tricks was to have you kneel on a nakryci, which was a small stick like a broom handle, put it behind your knees, and then clamp down on it. If you sit on that long enough, you lose all circulation in your legs, you'll get gangrene and you'll lose your legs. It generally didn't happen that way. Generally, a guy could only stand it so long then he'd roll off this and fall over. They would beat on him with a stick until he got back up on it. We had a lot of winter time and they'd make you sit out there in your shorts. Every once in a while with a cold wind blowing off the bay, they'd come out and throw a bucket of water on you. Chances were you would die of pneumonia. They'd beat on you regularly so you had several good chances of getting gangrene in your legs, or you could die of pneumonia out there in that cold without any clothes. Or you could just plain get beat to death for falling over too many times. Your chances of surviving were pretty bad. I remember seeing one guy out there almost two weeks. We'd go by on our way to work and many guys said that they wished they'd just kill him and get it over with. As I said, the guard was proceeding to walk me to the guard house and I have no idea how many times he asked but I know it was four or five times. He said, "Is the guard house alright?" and I would repeat, "Yes" and so we would proceed. We finally got 50 to 100 feet from the guard house and he stopped and asked me one more time and I said no again. Whether he believed me, or maybe he had a little bit of compassion, but he gave me a few whaps and let me go. I figured that was one of those deals again where I was saved from almost certain death.

One of the first things that happened when I came there was I had an operation, and so that took me to the end of October before I was back to work again. Then I went to the mine and worked a couple of months on the jack hammer crew. I suppose by this time we were close to Christmas. At Christmas time, we had a little celebration. I don't know if it was New Year's Day or Christmas Day. I remember some talk about it. We all had a day off and they gave us a better than usual meal and there were some speeches by our people that maybe this would be our last year, and as it turned out, it was.

As we got closer to the end of the war, we were bombed and had some pretty exciting incidents. When we saw the first B-29s come over, we were thrilled. They were great enormous airplanes. I had never seen a B-29 and I thought maybe they were Russian planes or something. They came in low over the town to bomb, the anti-aircraft guns starting firing at the planes and as they did, some Navy fighter planes that had been escorting them attacked the anti-aircraft guns, which made a very exciting event for us. We had so long ago ended our part of the war and spent these years as prisoners, and now were beginning to see the end and victory for the United States, which we'd always planned on but seemed so far away. It made us feel good, the coming victory and end of all this degradation. These little happy events were a thrill to us and let us know we were in fact winning the war. We'd look at these people and say that one of these days I'll be out of here, wearing my wrist watch again and my ring, and you guys will still be here. One time we heard the bombers coming and the guard was running around and jumping up and down and yelling. He could talk pretty good English and he said, "Run, run, run. The enemy is already here." We got a great kick out of that because we didn't think about it as being the enemy. We were just pretty doggone thrilled that they were coming and we could hear that old Texas motor oil again. We didn't consider them the enemy, even though they might drop a bomb on us. They came once with their bombs and almost burned down our camp. The bombs fell all over the camp and it was hard for me to believe, but the guys were hollering, "Burn this place. Burn it. Burn it to the ground." I was wondering where I was going to stay next winter. I didn't know there wasn't going to be a next winter, but as long as I'd been there I couldn't count on there not being another

---

137

winter. I sure didn't want to be sleeping out in the cold in that country in the middle of the winter, but it turned out alright. It certainly was fun to see those great enormous incendiary bombs banging and burning things. After all, they were the enemy, and when the enemy lost this war, we could go home.

There's an old saying that soldiers always use, "Some bullet's got my number on it." One of these incendiary bombs fell right outside the front gate and was laying there on the ground. It didn't go off. We'd walk by to look at it and on the side of it was a number. It had one of our guy's numbers. It was 12 something. I don't remember whose number it was, but there was his number on the bomb and the guy is looking at it and it had his number. He said, "Well, I'm one of the guys that saw a shell with my number on it." In any case, it didn't go off.

We'd see the B-29s coming and we'd really get a kick out of it. We were down in a shelter one time, heard the B-29s coming, and the guards standing outside would run us down into the holes and lock the doors. The guards were standing outside and we listened to them talking to the other guard. He saw B-29s coming and counted them. "Hyaku" means 100 and he said, "Hyaku etch, Hyaku nee, Hyaku son, Hyaku see." He's saying, "Hundred, hundred and one, hundred and two, oh darn." This really gave us a big thrill. We could hear those enormous B-29s going to do their job to end this war and get us home. It was a real pleasure to hear those poor old Japanese saying, "Oh wow." It was a great feeling to feel that America was really coming and that America was mighty and to see the might of the American Air Force. You just can't believe the wonderful feeling it gave us. They asked us one day when we saw them coming, "Are those your friends?" and you know, that was an interesting question. You didn't know how to answer it so we told him, "Yes, they're Americans." One gift they'd give us was a little bun or something and then they'd say, "big gift." So we told them, "big gift." Quite often when they'd be real concerned about it we'd say, yes, war was bad and of course it was. They were the ones that started it and they were the ones who captured us and drug us off to Japan so we couldn't be too disappointed with their losing.

My very good friend, Bill Milliken from Sabinal, Texas, we were together the entire time. In fact, Milliken was in my outfit, the 34th Pursuit Squadron. While we were on the farm in the Philippines, we worked together and we talked and visited. We spent many hours and days talking about sometime when we would be home again and what we'd do and wouldn't do. Milliken was a little older than I and he would tell me a lot of things I didn't really understand as a young man. He would tell me as an older man about dreams I'd have about what I was going to do when I came back to the States. We were buddies and we went to Japan together and were in Camp 17 together. Milliken didn't eat too good. He had kind of a thing about what he liked to eat and what he didn't, which was no help to him. Like everybody else, he was losing weight and getting weaker, I suppose since he was a little older. One day he went by the place where they kept the ashes of the dead and he said to me, "Hamilton, I don't know whether we're tough enough," but we were. I thought of that many times since then. We fought a long hard battle and we were tough. Poor old Milliken was reaching the end of his rope. That spring he got sick and went in the hospital and I went over to visit him. I'd stop in and visit him for a little bit every once in a while after work. He just didn't seem to be improving and was getting weaker and weaker. One morning after work I came by, went to his bed and he was dead. I didn't know whether anybody else had even noticed or not. I went on. I didn't say anything to anyone. Old Milliken was gone. He'd fought the good fight and now it was over.

Maps of Japan (Note location of Nagaski)

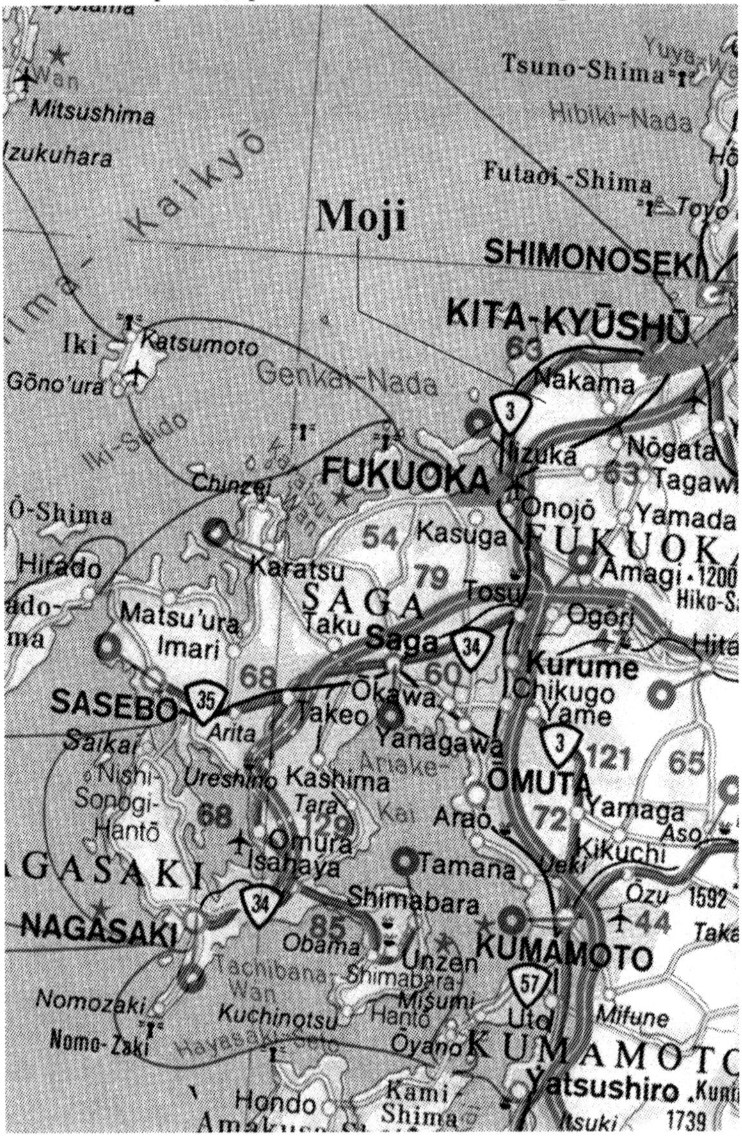

Omuta (my camp#17)

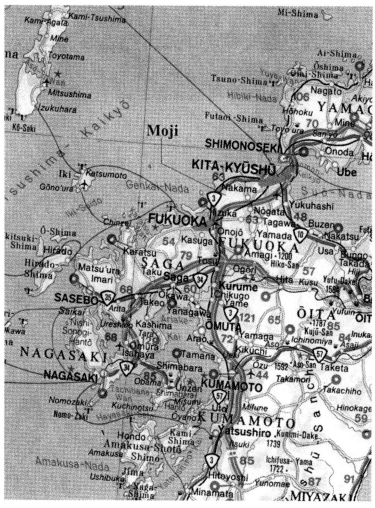

Moji (my landing site)

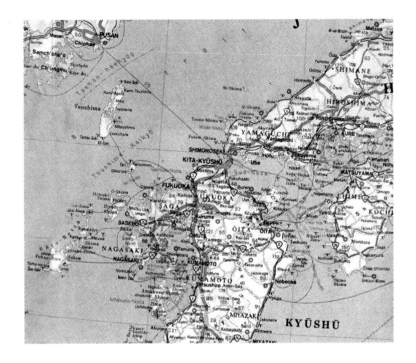

Hiroshima

Chapter Fourteen

THE WAR'S END, VICTORY AT LAST

Spring went into summer, summer finally came to August, and one day it happened. When we left the mine they said it was a big holiday and we marched back to the camp. The big rumor around camp was the war was over but nobody would say anything. We took the day off and that night we all talked about it and wondered. The next day they said, "No work today either." So we thought more and more that maybe the war really was over. The third day came and still no work and we thought, "Wow, this has got to be it. The war must surely be over." Some guys still didn't believe it. With all the big and wonderful things and the big and terrible things of the past, it was difficult to believe it all happened. After the third day we got the word for all of us to assemble in the center of the field and someone was going to talk to us. We went out and the camp commander came out. He went up on the platform where we had our roll call, our tinko, and he said, "I have good news for you. The hostilities have ceased. Let us all be friends." Well, we thought that was a big joke. He wouldn't have allowed the hostilities to cease if he had anything to do with it. It was great to say let's be friends after the way they treated us, but anyway it was all over and everybody was happy. We didn't know what to think. Here we were, him telling us the war is over, and we're still in camp and no Americans are here. We wanted to know what was going to happen. We sat there a few days and one day some B-29s came over. I believe they were B-29s, but I'm not absolutely sure. They had their bomb bay doors opened and dropped cases and cases of food and barrels and barrels of food. They were just flying out of the sky. The great big colorful parachutes would come open; it was so exciting. There were about 40 cases of food and some of these fell completely apart, and when you looked at the sky you would see 40 cases of canned food headed for you. When these great big 60-gallon barrels would hit the end of that parachute rope, they'd break through the rope and you'd see them coming down towards you. It turned out to be pretty wild. In fact, one case of peaches hit and killed one of the boys. We had all these big electrical wires that I mentioned before that ran through the camps. These barrels and cases of food were hitting these wires and snapping them, and they were whirling around and curling up and throwing sparks all over the place. I tell you it was something wild. One of the 60-gallon barrels came through a barracks. The old Dutch chaplain was laying over there on his bed in the corner and one of the barrels came through one side of the barracks and went right out the other side. He came running out of his place and said, "These Japs have been trying to kill me for three and a half years and the Americans are going to do it now." Mostly it was a happy, exciting, and wonderful time. We got these beautiful colored parachutes and put them up in between our barracks. The sun shone through them, red, white and blue. We discussed the implication of whose country was represented because of the colors of the parachutes, but I'm sure the colors were accidental. However, they were very pretty and we set them up like tents in between the barracks and some of the food we salvaged was stacked in between the barracks. It was a fabulous time. They made two or three drops to us. Some were better than others and some of the barrels tore big holes in the back fence. Here we were with big holes in the back

fence and all the guards slipped out of camp. We collected
everything they left. We got their rifles and set up as if it
were our own camp. Some of us went through the holes in
the fence and walked around the town. That was an absolutely incredible feeling to know we were free. We stayed at
the camp and about the 22nd of the month, I believe, a man
from the *Chicago Sun* came in and told us about the atomic
bomb. It was the first time we knew about the atomic bomb.
I think I'd better say here that this is a part of my story I kind
of overlooked. I did see the Nagasaki atomic bomb and didn't
know what it was at the time. When we came out of the shel-
ters and looked over in that direction, we saw this great
enormous billowing cloud way up as high as you could see. It
was beginning to slowly drift off to the north of us and we
thought, "Nagasaki must have sure been hit today." The man
from the *Chicago Sun* told us our military was down at Kanoya.
The Americans had come in and seized the southern-most
airbase at Kanoya, and those were the only Americans on our
island. He said if we wanted to get down there, they were
using Kanoya as an airbase and all kinds of planes were flying
supplies in every day and going back to the Philippines empty.
So if we'd get down there, we could fly to the Philippines
and be on our way home. We didn't know what to do about
this. Lt. Cdr. Little (Navy) was in charge of our camp and
said this was now an Army camp, he was the commander and
nobody could leave. If anybody did, they would be court
martialed. Most people had very little use for Lt. Cdr. Little.
He had been a very controversial man, but that was beside
the point. We weren't going to have anybody tell us where
we were going to stay. Lt. Cdr. Little had stationed a guard
down by the train station to see that nobody left. I went down
to the train station with about 150 guys and the guard he
stationed down there went with us. The train came in and we
told them we wanted to get on it. They told us there wasn't
any room. We told them not to worry, we'd find room and got

145

on. That was a wild ride in the middle of the night. I don't know where we were, but we came into an old station somewhere and another train came into the station, and I'm sure our conductor really wanted to get rid of us. He told us the train that was in the station was the one we should be on. So, we jumped down and ran over to the other train and the guy on the other train told us no, that we were on the wrong train, that the other train was right. So we ran back and started to jump back on the other train and about that time a guard ran up to my window and stood there holding his bayonet like he was going to stab me. I said, "Bacaro" which means fool. He backed off and I ran and jumped on the train and we were off.

Before the train ride, while we were in the camp waiting for something to happen, some of the guys said to me, "Hey, let's go down to Fukuoka." I thought that would be kind of fun. It's a big town down the way and there was another prison camp and we could go down and visit the other guys. So, five other guys and I went downtown and of course the Japanese were still in complete command. They still had their army on the streets, armed soldiers and armed guards. Their high ranking officers had priority at trains. The trains were terribly crowded but we used our own initiative. We went to a place where the important people seemed to be getting in so we stepped ahead of them and got on the train. They stood back and let us so we pulled a big bluff and took off on the train. We were tearing along on this train down through the country and the train was so crowded. Every time we would stop at a station the people would see us and you could see that they were really shaken. They realized they were seeing the real live enemy. We arrived at Fukuoka and it was unbelievable. The town was virtually burned down. In a lot of places, about all you could see were big safes setting around in what had been a building. There was a train station of sorts still there. Across from the train station was Kim Pe headquarters. Kim

Pe headquarters in Japan was kind of like Gestapo headquarters. They were the police that everybody dreaded, the big heavy national police headquarters. So, one of the guys said, "Let's go over to Kim Pe headquarters and find out where the camp is." I was pretty leery about that. I didn't want to mess with those guys because they were the bad people. We went over to Kim Pe headquarters and there were a bunch of high ranking officers standing around looking their best in slick uniforms and big swords. I felt a little shaky and was afraid something bad was going to happen. One of the guys said, "We want an interpreter right now." They gave us a cold stare, followed by a bunch of chatter, and in just a little bit we had an interpreter. At about the same time, this embarrassing pause came. Six Navy fighter planes made a low-level pass right over the town. Those planes reminded them they had lost the war. The interpreter drew us a map and showed us where to get on the street car. The guy running the street car caught hold of me by the collar. He just grabbed hold of me and said, "You have to pay." I said, "No, we're Americans. Americans own this whole country. We work for MacArthur and MacArthur said that soldiers pay for nothing. This is not Japan, it's the United States." There was no more argument. He didn't say anything else. We rode on the street car and paid nothing.

We got off at the prison camp and it was beautiful. There was a lovely park with flags flying on tall poles. They had taken these splendid looking parachutes that I told about and cut them into streamers and put them on long poles out in front of the camp. I mean that camp was pretty. They were in pine trees with grass. It was really nice. There was a guard marching up and down in front with his rifle on his shoulder. We were a little leery and hollered to the guys in the camp, "What's the deal with the guard?" One said, "Oh, don't worry about him. He just hasn't gotten the word yet." We visited for a time and returned to our camp.

Now I'm back on the train where we changed trains in the middle of the night. We're going to Kanoya. It was quite a trip. We arrived at a beautiful beach. The train stopped at this seaside area with beautiful waves coming ashore. It was a resort area. We got off of the train and some of the guys went out and got into the water. The ocean was rolling up. Gosh, you thought you were in southern California. In fact, some of the guys went out and almost drowned. In a little bit, we got back on the train and took off again. Finally, we came into Kanoya. It was a little station. We had finally arrived. We pull into the station, got off the train and there's a real American guard standing there. I suppose you could say that's when I returned to military control. There was an MP standing at the station and a beer truck there. So all the guys said, "Hey, a beer truck." They jumped off and started taking beer off the truck. The guard said, "You can't drink that Japanese beer." The guys didn't pay any attention to him. About that time, a jeep came tearing up with a Major in it and slid to a stop. He said, "Those guys can't drink this beer." The guard said to the Major, "What am I going to do? Do you want me to shoot them?" The Major shook his head, got back into his jeep and took off. It was a marvelous party. Soon we were in the camp walking around and we came to a place where there were guards that had some Japanese prisoners working for them. Suddenly, just like that, the whole situation was reversed. It was hard to believe. We're the winners. We're the victors. The war is over. Everything's reversed and we've got Japanese prisoners. We stopped and had a bit of conversation with the guards. They told us, "We can't get these Japanese to work." One of our boys said, "What do you mean, they're not going to work? That's the most ridiculous thing I've ever heard of. Loan me that gun of yours." The guard had a grease gun type machine gun and one of the guys grabbed the gun, walked over to where the Japanese prisoners were and told them that he'd been a prisoner of the Japanese for three and a half years and had seen thousands of his buddies die. If they didn't get on the ball and start working real fast, he'd just be happy to see a lot of Japanese die. I tell you, there was a lot of work going on real quick. I don't know if that proves anything. Here was the old deal again. They'd treated us like dogs and we'd suffered for three and a half years. Just as soon as they're the prisoners they think they're going to get away with doing what they want. They're the badies now. I don't know what the moral of the story is, except it was a real pleasure for us to see those guys stepping lively for a change instead of us.

Chapter Fifteen

THE HAPPY ROAD HOME

Anyway, we were in Kanoya, checked in, returned to military control and had a good old state-side meal. We're back with our people. It's all over. The day of redemption has arrived. We have been saved; we're in a new world. Happiness is everywhere. It was hard to believe. Just incredible. It's something that we've many times thought would never happen. The thing we always waited for, we lived for, in eternal hope. We always lived with the hope that someday at the end of the line, somewhere, sometime, we'd be back home, and me, wearing my wrist watch and my ring and having a job and it finally happened.

They put us on a plane and we flew to Okinawa. We landed in Okinawa and in a few minutes Red Cross people came out and gave us hot chocolate, doughnuts, cokes and stuff like that. We were there for a few minutes, I don't know, 20 or 30 minutes. We milled around and stretched our legs a little bit. When they told us it was time to go again we got back on our planes and left. I remember circling into the Philippines. It was the beautiful green Philippines down below us again, the banana trees and the palm trees. Good old Philippines. Here we were, back again. We slowly circled in for a landing and were taken to the 29th Replacement Depot. It was south of Manila somewhere. It was a real nice place with beautiful vegetation, green, nice, everything was wonderful. They had all kinds of tents set up and a special place for the prisoners. They said they had issued double rations and there'd be more than any of us could possibly eat. We could eat whatever we wanted and when we wanted. We wouldn't be required to do any kind of work and would be given physical examinations. They set up a canteen for us with candy bars and cokes and things like that absolutely free. You'd just go over and get what you want. You didn't have to pay for anything. We were really living. I tell you, we were suddenly transferred from another world into heaven. We'd come to a wonderful, wonderful end to our life in prison. It was a great day. We stayed there a couple of weeks and we really had it nice. We laid around in tents and went to movies at night. We hadn't seen movies in years. One day we were laying around in our tent and the guys hadn't policed things up much. A lieutenant came by and the guys were eating candy bars and throwing papers on the floor and stuff like that, and he said, "I know you guys aren't supposed to have to do any kind of work, but I think you would feel ashamed of yourselves, living so messy." We all thought that was funny. It was a wonderful feeling to be not only back, not only safe, but we're a special class. We're getting special treatment. I tell you for sure, I really appreciated it. It was wonderful. We were notified that everybody would get one promotion in rank. They found out that because I was a 1st 3rd, I'd been carried as an E-4 for all the time I'd been prison, so I was automatically eligible for Staff Sgt. or E-5. The orders came out and I was promoted to corporal. That was about the same time we got orders to get on the boat and go home. I had my shipping orders home, we received new uniforms, new combat boots and so forth. I still have the combat boots. In any case, I was promoted to corporal and I was to sail as a corporal. I said, "Is there anything I can do about that?" They said, "Well, you can stay here, get it changed and catch a later boat." I said, "No, I'll just go home." We got on our boat and sailed for the United States. We had a nice ship and sailed down through the San Bernadino Straits, south of the Philippines. As we passed through the deepest parts of the Pacific Ocean, the captain of the ship came on the loud speaker and told us of the great naval battles that had gone on in the San Bernadino Straits. We sank the greater portion of the Japanese fleet as it passed through the San Bernadino Straits during the battle of Leyte. We were passing through almost the exact areas where the great Japanese ships had been sunk. We proceeded on and traveled toward Hawaii. Things went along nice. We enjoyed everything. We were in our glory and had preferential treatment. We were told we didn't have to do any kind of work. We were supposed to do nothing until we had physical examinations and then they would decide whether we would return to active duty. We could buy candy bars and everything. I bought a whole box of 24 solid milk chocolate candy bars, sat down and ate them all. I have no idea why it didn't kill me. It didn't even make me sick. Anyway, we sailed on and enjoyed this wonderful trip and eventually we arrived in Seattle. As we passed through Puget Sound at night, boats came out from Seattle and came alongside. They had music, dancing girls, beautiful lights and all sorts of welcoming deals to welcome us home. It was really a marvelous feeling. You could see that people were out there welcoming us home. It was a wonderful, wonderful, wonderful feeling.

We were moved to Madigan General Hospital, where we were to get a physical evaluation to find out what our situation was. Looking back on that time, it's been said they weren't nearly thorough enough when giving us our physical examinations, particularly as it pertained to mental stresses and three and a half years of prisoner-type life. Many of our veterans were left with practically no record of what condition they were in when they came home. We were all in total euphoria. We were happy. We had won the war. The Japanese had lost. We were glorious victors. It was all over. Everybody was happy. Who worried about anything? So, you certainly weren't in any mood to try to analyze your physical condition be it pro or con. You just wanted to get home and later, if you had any physical problems, you figured somebody would fix them. What's the big deal? It was all kind of glossed over. Anyway, they were very nice to us in Madigan General Hospital. I stayed there two weeks and several times I was told by people who knew what they were talking about, "Gee, if you want to go home, why don't you just go?" What were we there for? In fact, I said that we really needed a little better evaluation, not less. We finally received our orders and I and 13 other guys were to go to Ft. Leavenworth, Kansas. I still was a corporal. I hadn't gotten my staff sergeant rating. yet. I went again and asked about getting my staff sergeant stripes and here I had orders as a corporal to get on the train. Finally, they gave me my staff sergeant rank but my orders to get on the train were still as a corporal. So I went on the train with my corporal rank and my corporal orders because I wasn't officially shipped out as a staff sargent. I found out the 13 guys I was with, if I'd had my E5 or my staff sergeant rank, I'd have been the senior NCO on the train. After we started toward Ft. Leavenworth, over half the guys jumped off. They got close to their homes and just said, "See you later guys." and got off the train and went home. That would have really shaken me up as a responsible NCO. No telling what kind of emotional upset I would have been in if I had been in charge with everybody going AWOL on me. Since I wasn't in charge, I didn't worry about it. We got into Ft. Leavenworth and it didn't make any difference. Nobody cared that much. We got to Leavenworth and reported in. The Captain there said, "Where are the other guys?" We said, "They went home." He said, "Home? Don't they know they're AWOL?" We said, "Don't talk to us. We're here." He calmed down. It turned out that nobody did anything about those people going home. The last thing in the world they

153

wanted to do was courtmartial a guy for going home after being a prisoner of war for three and a half years and a veteran of Bataan and Corregidor. They would have been laughed out of town if they would have tried to courtmartial a poor guy like that.

At Ft. Leavenworth, it was good old Army chow again. Anything we didn't have, we received. We got orders to go on 90-day TDY (temporary duty) at home. I got my 90-day TDY at home orders and caught a train and went to Salina, Kansas. I might regress there just a little bit and say why I went to Salina. When I got to Madigan General, we got a free phone call home and I called home and found out my parents were now living in Wichita. I talked to my mother and brother and his new wife and found out that Jean, a girl I knew before the war, was in Salina. In the meantime, I got a letter from her. She found out I was at Madigan General and before I left Madigan General, I got a letter from Jean. We'd been very good friends before the war and I was very anxious to see her. I got off the train in Salina and found Jean. She was living with her folks and I visited with her. I had an interesting little incident here. I went over to visit with my Uncle Lloyd and I say hello to my Aunt Mary. Lloyd called me aside and told me that it wasn't my aunt Mary I'd been talking to, it was aunt Emma. Aunt Mary had passed on and he had married Emma. They were sisters and I'd been gone so long, I didn't recognize the difference. Anyway, I was home. It was a wonderful feeling and a wonderful time. Within a few weeks, Jean and I were married and we went back to my folks in Wichita.

That was the end of my great adventure. Now I've completed the story I wanted to write for so many years about what happened to me in World War II as a veteran of Bataan and Corregidor, as a veteran of three and a half years in a Japanese prison camp, of my survival under unbelievable conditions, of my opportunity to have been in on a great epic of history, to have seen the atomic bomb at Nagasaki, to have had the opportunity to see the great Japanese fleet sitting in anchor in Manila Bay, to stand in the midst of a great Japanese Army in the middle of their attacks under battlefield conditions, to have had the opportunity to stand on the beaches and watch as our troops made a magnificent defense of the beaches and turn away 30 barges with 3,000 to 3,500 Japanese, to actually have been engaged on the beaches with 700 of the crack Japanese commandos of General Homa's top overseas troops. I felt privileged to have seen all of these things; to watch the great sweep of the Japanese Army across the Philippines; to see our people rise to heroic levels, the magnificent efforts they made in spite of their lack of supplies; to see them act as real soldiers, as real men, and make a fantastic defense of the Philippines which held up, for a considerable time, the great Japanese Army. I feel this whole experience for me – —a time of degradation, a time of great shortage of food, nutrition and suffering from vitamin deficiencies which may have affected my life forever – —I view it as a great opportunity and a great time in my life. I don't know what to say other than that this is the end of my story and the beginning of a new life. I had won my personal war with Japan. I had faced them on the battlefield. I had faced them on the death march. I had faced them on the prison ships and in their death camps. When the final end came, they had done their worst and I was still alive.

Jeannie and I were married and I began a career in the Air Force of 29 years. We raised five wonderful children and I feel that Jean and I had a wonderful life in the Air Force followed by eight more years of civil service.

I want to dedicate this especially to Jeannie, all my children and grandchildren and generations to come of my future descendants. I want them to be able to, if they wish, go back and say, "Well, Grandpa was there." They can say, "Well, sure. Here's his story." Thank you and good-bye.

Conversation With My Son

My son Robert, who lives in Montana, said, "Your story is good, Dad. It's a great book but you left out the real part, the part you could not tell any of us kids, because not only were we too young to understand, we were too young to fathom the depth man can sink to in his quest for power over others. As an adult, I have read in other books the things you could not tell us or write about. I understand your reservations about reliving that hideous time and putting it down on paper. Maybe I'm asking too much, but your story, as you tell it, is so full of wonder and love; of the simplest moments of living we all take for granted; of moments of joy and humor in those degrading years, without hope of deliverance; of values lost or held in abeyance because your world had lost its mind. We need to know the worst of it in order to fully evaluate the courage and bravery you were blessed with as your eyes saw and your body felt the wrath of your captors. Dad, tell the real story for those who did not come back. Tell why they did not return and why we must not let something like this happen ever again—an addendum to your story, short by necessity, because in the telling the images become so real again it can only be endured briefly and reverently. Tell them, Dad."

I said, "Son, maybe you're right. I think I'll just write it down and let the reader know why I could not fill in my story with the literal truth of those years. It is almost beyond belief, but I'll try my best for as long as I can."

I've already given the enormous numbers of those who fell during the death march, died at Camp O'Donnell, died at Cabauatuan, on the hell ships, and in the Japanese prisons. More American POWs died in those Phillippine prisons than in any foreign prisons before or since.

When I was moved into Hospital #2 in the dysentery area with nine other men, within two weeks those nine were dead. I was in different wards with different diseases for one year and as far as I know, I was the only man to come out of those wards during that time alive.

Every morning when I woke up, five to seven men would be dead from malaria or dysentery or for many other reasons. The men lay on filthy straw with their mouths open, green blow flies crawling in and out while their last gasps of life drifted away. All night long, I would listen to them struggle for their last breath. Some died from just plain neglect, no name attached as a reason for their death; some just gave up. Did you know that you can sit down, close your eyes and be dead in 10 minutes or three days, and no one will notice until you are covered with flies and fail to brush them off? Then that body, along with many others, may not be buried for four days, because those still living do not have the energy to drag the bodies out and dig holes in the hard ground.

The slit trenches that served as latrines were so full of bloody defecation that sometimes, a body fell in. The men were fighting to eat their pitiful rations of sloppy rice, unable to keep dozens of blow flies off their mess kit. At the slit trenches, men struggled to stand and the trails back to the barracks would be sloppy with their bloody defecation. Other men walking on those same trails would slip in their bare feet and fall, needing help to stand again.

I was so weak, I could not step over a two-by-four doorsill. I had to turn sideways and slide my feet over the sill. I had pellagra blisters two or three inches across my legs and hands. People with beri beri were swollen up like huge fat people, their testicles sometimes as large as volleyballs and their penises as big as a large sausage. Generally, they swelled until they burst; their bodily fluids drained out of them, and they died. Sometimes, the skin on their legs would split open and they would die of infection.

People developed large ulcers as big as a baseball all over their bodies. I saw ulcers over the spine and could see the actual vertebrae sticking out while they died a slow, miserable death. I came down with dyptheria and when I entered the hospital ward, I was told they had already had 200 men die from the disease. It generally blocks the throat and the person chokes to death. I lay and listened most of one night to a man from my hometown slowly choke to death. Starting about midnight, his gasps became more and more labored until it was finally over about three in the morning. I sat leaning against the building for three hours, a pleasant night, the stars shining clear and beautiful, heard his last gasp, and then silence.

In the Zero Ward that no one expected to leave alive, the most likely to die in the night were lined up in the order of expected deaths. Sometimes it was called "St. Peter's Ward." I was there and I came out alive. How or why, I will never know.

The hell ship I was on took 62 days to get to Japan. There were a thousand men on board with nowhere to sit upright or even lay down. When the hatches were closed, the heat was horrible; it cut out the light and air. At night, no one was allowed to go topside to go to the toilet. We had five gallon cans in the middle of the floor and when they were full, they just ran over. We tried to stay as far away from them as possible so the liquid would not run over or on us. We lay in the dark, wondering how many days, weeks or months we would be on this horrible ship. We finally made it to Japan, and strange as it seems, life got a little better. But, my story tells that part.

I could tell more, Robert, but I can't bear the images any

longer. All of this did happen and by the grace of God, I somehow survived. I don't think the reader should have to visualize any more degradation of his fellow man, either. Suffice to say, man can endure the most horrible things and still come out whole on the other side. If people are repulsed by what I've written, it is unfortunate, but this is only a small part of a long, unbearable period of terror, misery and death. Let us all vow to never let it happen again, and live our lives with gratitude for our beautiful country and all the freedoms we enjoy under the protection of our armed forces and the flag so many have died to protect.

This, my son, is my part of the real story. You were right, it did need to be told. It needed to be told from memory so memory will not become fiction. Memory is tiny when seen through the large end of a telescope. I hope I am preserving memory and all of its spirits, which have been wandering through my mind. Memory is selective and imperfect, yet as an antique it has lasting qualities, especially when pulled from a shelf and read, because memory has need of help.

AMI

Picture of Weldon Hamilton in the Air Force
February 21, 1957

Picture of Weldon Hamilton addressing the troops at White Sand Missile Range, NM

BIOGRAPHY

Mr. Weldon C. Hamilton joined the U.S. Army Air Corps on October 5, 1940. He was shipped to the Philippines in November of 1941.

He fought in the Battle of Bataan, a battle that the Japanese planned to win in three weeks, but required four months instead. When food and ammunition ran out, Bataan was overrun.

Mr. Hamilton was taken prisoner of war by the Japanese. He made the infamous Death March. On the Death March, over 10,000 men died. He was held for 1,256 days. He was held in the Philippines for over two years, first in Camp O'Donnell, where over 25,000 men died in less than two months. He was then held in Camp Cabanatuan, where 3,000 died, the most Americans ever to die in an overseas prison camp, and second only to Andersonville in all of our history. He was then taken to Japan on one of the notorious "hell ships." At the end of the war, he was 30 miles from Nagasaki, where he witnessed the dropping of the Nagasaki atomic bomb.

He continued on in the Air Force and retired as a Chief Warrant Officer CWO-4 in 1969. He has many decorations, including The Presidential Unit Citation with two oak leaf clusters and the Bronze Star.

CPSIA information can be obtained at www.ICGtesting.com
Printed in the USA
BVOW040244011012

301683BV00001B/2/A